WHOSE PAST IS IT ANYWAY?

THE ULSTER COVENANT,
THE EASTER RISING
& THE BATTLE OF
THE SOMME

Jude Collins

The
History
Press
Ireland

To – who else? – Maureen, Phoebe, Patrick, Matt and Hugh

'There are two tragedies in life. One is to lose your heart's desire.
The other is to gain it.' George Bernard Shaw

First published 2012

The History Press Ireland
119 Lower Baggot Street
Dublin 2
Ireland
www.thehistorypress.ie

© Jude Collins, 2012

The right of Jude Collins to be identified as the Author
of this work has been asserted in accordance with the
Copyrights, Designs and Patents Act 1988.

British Library Cataloguing in Publication Data.
A catalogue record for this book is available from the British Library.

ISBN 978 1 84588 754 4

Typesetting and origination by The History Press
Printed in Great Britain

CONTENTS

INTRODUCTION

In one way, marking centenaries makes little sense. Why one hundred? We could as easily focus on a 99th or a 101st anniversary, and with as much validity. Even on a personal level, the singling out of particular events for anniversary attention – your birthday, my wedding day, the date of someone's death – is odd. But maybe understandable. We humans feel a need to impose shape on experience, to link the past with the present, to look for pointers that help us understand what has happened and what significance we should attach to it. Without an anniversary to mark an event, there's a danger it could become blurred or lost in the thicket of other happenings, that danger increasing with the passage of time. And so we choose particular points, erect milestones on the road that tell us where we were and who we are.

Ireland, in 2012, is entering into what some have called 'the decade of centenaries'. There are a lot of them: the Ulster Covenant, the Dublin Lock-out, the Larne gun-running, the Howth gun-running, the First World War, the Easter Rising, the Tan War, the Truce, the Civil War, partition. Each of these events makes its own contribution to our history, and each relates to the others, not just through proximity in time, but because it builds on or reacts against others.

This book takes three of these centenaries for consideration. The Ulster Covenant saw the unionist people in Ulster solemnly commit themselves to all measures to block the passage of the London Government's Home Rule Bill. Randolph Churchill encouraged them in their stand, declaring that 'the Orange card would be the one to play'. And so it proved. Then came 1914, and the Ulster Volunteers, established to resist Britain's Home Rule intentions for Ireland, marched in support of Britain to the carnage of the Somme – as did thousands of Irishmen from the south. The third centenary looked at here, Easter 1916, is the seminal event of modern Irish republicanism. From its apparent failure came a measure of Irish independence, with the creation in 1922 of a twenty-six-county Free State.

History, we're told, is written by the victors. The interviews in this book are with people of different political allegiances who see our shared history differently. Some approach the centenaries with caution or even apprehension, fearing the possibility of deepened division in Ireland; more see the potential of these commemorations to speak to our present situation and add to our understanding. Some believe these centenaries should be occasions for the honouring of the dead; others argue for reflection on the events, in the belief that new meanings for today may be found in what happened 100 years ago.

In a few interviews, one can detect a suspicion that commemorations may be manipulated. Jim Allister cautions against the possibility that the centenaries of these three events will be seized by different factions and ownership claimed, because they fear that otherwise the contrast with their own actions – or inaction – might become too glaring. Others, like Mary Lou McDonald, see the centenaries as an opportunity for joint commemoration. Others again, notably Ian Paisley Jr, stress the need to see each event in its historical context.

Granted that we owe a debt to the past, does the meaning of that past change with the passage of time? A recurrent theme among those interviewed was the degree of understanding the past might offer the present, and the extent to which the past shapes our future. Bernadette McAliskey is alert to the danger that the present may become prisoner to the past and is robust in her challenge of such confinement. Other interviewees remark on the need to interrogate the past in order to understand it anew; time changes the meaning events have for us, but only when we are prepared to question them closely. Common sense tells us that our generation sees events from a more distant vantage point than those who participated in them, and this can show what happened in a different light. Some interviewees avoid this kind of emphasis. They believe our debt to the past is a straightforward one: these were people who performed great deeds and it is fitting we recognise with gratitude what has been done for us. Roddy Doyle, in contrast, calls for a humanising of the figures from the past: we must learn to see the mighty dead as mortal beings like ourselves, not as mythic figures.

Few of the interviewees, with the exception of Eoghan Harris, offer much in the way of commemoration specifics. Where it occurs, it is more usually in a negative form: we must avoid any militarisation or triumphalism in our celebrations, for example. Harris outlines a number of practical schemes which he believes would allow people from the north to become more familiar with those from the south and vice versa – a sort of mass education programme. Harris is particularly emphatic on the role of television in commemoration and urges government intervention, north and south, so that this may happen in an effective manner.

The reader may be surprised by the level of optimism in this book. Different political traditions may lay claim to different centenaries, but most interviewees look forward in hope, believing these occasions will provide opportunities in which understanding outweighs any possible danger. None of those interviewed believed that the centenaries need drag us back to the conflict from which Ireland has lately emerged. The belief is rather that the centenaries offer a chance for fresh thinking about the past and what it says to us.

My sincere thanks to all those who contributed so generously of their time in the composition of this book. It is my hope that the views expressed here will provide a stimulus for discussion and debate in the coming days and years, and that the distinguishing features of that debate will be honesty and respect.

Jude Collins
March 2012

EOGHAN HARRIS

*Eoghan Harris is a journalist, columnist and political commentator.
He currently writes for the* Sunday Independent. *He was a
member of Seanad Éireann from 2007 to 2011, having been
nominated by the An Taoiseach, Bertie Ahern.*

Background

The house I grew up in was probably the most political house in Ireland – none of my friends had a house like that. My grandfather would visit every Sunday. He'd been an intelligence officer in the First Cork Brigade, and had been out in 1916, but more important than that, he was older than most of the Irish Volunteers in Cork. He had been a founding member of the Gaelic League in Cork with Terence McSwiney and MacCurtain, and MacCurtain was a very close friend of his. He didn't have that much time for McSwiney; he thought he was a bit of a wimp, to be straight about it. He hated both the Free State and de Valera indiscriminately.

He was a solicitor's clerk and they held onto him after 1916 pretty well, but his eyesight came against him. There were jobs in Cork Corporation given to fellahs with disabilities, but he couldn't get one because he wouldn't take the oath of allegiance. Then when de Valera came in, he hated de Valera as well, so he remained a kind of intransigent republican.

My father was more of a communist. He tried to get to Spain to fight in the civil war. He started a small business, but he remained a very hard-line radical republican and so it was inevitable that I would gravitate towards Sinn Féin.

In our house they talked non-stop. And it was detailed, hard-core stuff. Growing up I knew a lot of the Cork republicans who had been in the Coventry bombing campaign and that kind of thing – Jim Savage, Jim Donovan who was an explosives officer. Cork was full of former hardcore republicans.

When I was at university, I didn't spend much time in college; I spent most of my time downtown, and the Wolfe Tone Society in Dublin got in touch with us. We didn't know much about them. Roy Johnston came down once, and myself and Dáithí Ó Conaill, who later became chief-of-staff of the Provos, started a Wolfe Tone Society in Cork. We used to meet in the Father Mathew Hall, and on a wet night, when things were slow, there were only about seven of us there. There were two girls that I think we were half-interested in. On a slow night, the girls would ask Ó Conaill to show his back. He would do so reluctantly, but if we were stuck or bored, having had our meeting, he would take off his shirt. Down along his back were stitched the Sten gun bullets he had received on the northern raid. It was like a nightmare of a back, and how he breathed I don't know.

I liked Ó Conaill a lot; I got on very well with him. Our first activity was to plant flowers on the Western Road in Cork, to beautify the environs of the city coming in. We wanted to do something civic, and we set up a flower co-operative, which has flourished ever since.

But my first big march or demo: the Earl of Rosse was visiting Cork, and Barry took it into his head that he was somehow connected with an event in the War of Independence – he was very vague about it. Barry was wrong but I didn't care. Rosse was coming to Cork, and Barry had denounced the visit and called upon the people to boycott Rosse's visit to the Cork Choral Festival, as it was. Nobody took a bit of notice of Barry – he was old at that time and nearly blind. He lived in a flat above a beautiful part of Patrick Street; he could look down the Grand Parade and look up Patrick Street, so he could see the whole traffic of the city passing. And he called for a boycott. I don't know – I felt that I somehow owed him. I was a very good organiser and I organised the biggest march ever from UCC, of almost the entire student body – 98 per cent. It was done in total silence. We marched in fours past Barry's flat and he waved to us from the window as we made our way to City Hall.

I was sent up to Maghera, to one of the founding movements of the civil rights organisation. I was sent up because Roy Johnston had a terrible stutter and Tony Coughlan had written this document about the civil rights movement, and I was up there to drive Goulding when he wouldn't drive himself. The meeting was in Kevin Agnew's farmhouse. The northern command of the IRA were all there – Liam McMillen and McBirney from Belfast, Jim Sullivan from Belfast, and a whole lot more – and Francie Donnelly from the border. Then there was a big contingent of representatives from the communist party – I don't know if Fred Heatley was there but Betty Sinclair was. And they all read this document from Coughlan, which fundamentally was the organisational document of the civil rights movement.

So we started a series of peaceful marches. I remember the famous phrase in it that I had to read out, 'This whole strategy will fall apart at the first sound of a bomb or a bullet.' They didn't see that there could be other eventualities apart from that, such as maybe having civil rights marches broken up forcibly by other means.

Certainly after Bloody Sunday I was in a very militant mood and I can't honestly say that I had any warm feelings for the British Army.

I didn't, however, believe in an insurrection or armed struggle, because I didn't believe it was practical. I feared all sorts of things – that the border would be redrawn or something. In 1970, my whole reaction was, 'Don't let it happen down here, try and calm this situation down.' Then as the situation went along, in 1971 and 1972, I fell very much under the thinking of Conor Cruise O'Brien. We had our disagreements – I always remained a bit more republican – but fundamentally I agreed with him that the southern state had never faced the northern question fully and never understood it, and never really understood either the unionists or the nationalists. I said, 'What are we messing around with this for? We've no business dabbling in this.'

My position hardened over the years until finally, I suppose … I never was a two-nationist, but certainly I regard the northern settlement as the least of all evils. I didn't regard it as a good settlement, nor do I regard the current settlement in Northern Ireland as a very stable one, but I regarded it as the least of all possible evils and I wanted to keep the Republic away from all this stuff, because I thought the Republic was full of shit about Northern Ireland. If they were going to invade or they wanted a united country, they'd have to arm and prepare for it properly. They'd never done that, they just engaged in armchair rhetoric.

I describe myself as a revisionist republican. When I say that the state in the north is unstable, I don't think it'll disintegrate into violence or chaos. I mean not stable in the sense that it will evolve; it's not a permanent political settlement in my view. And I hope it will evolve towards a united Ireland, towards a federal Ireland. That's my position on it.

The Centenaries

I think the centenaries will receive a lot of public attention. I should point out that from 1966 onwards to the 1970s, and the split taking place, my thinking began to change very strongly. I became slowly but relentlessly very anti-nationalist. I feared a spilling of the northern conflict over the border and the Irish Army getting involved. And far from being sanguine about that, I thought the simple truth was that they'd get the shit kicked out of them – that's what bothered me. My fear was that there'd be a war, a civil war, and that we would lose! The Republic's Army wasn't up to that kind of stuff, nor the IRA. I just thought it was a very stupid kind of notion.

I regard the Ulster Covenant of 1912 as fundamentally a delinquent political act, like I regard the 1916 Rising as a delinquent political act. I regard both of these – and these are foundation events – as fundamentally very problematic. Now they're completely different to the Somme or the 1913 Lock-out. There are a lot of people trying to get in on these centenaries. The fact is 1912 and 1916 are mirror images of each other. Nineteen sixteen, in my view, was a reaction to the 1912 Covenant in many ways. It was what I call a delusionary reaction; Pearse and that bullshit about, you know, if the Ulstermen have guns in their hands, we should have guns in our hands – all that sort of rhetoric. Not understanding that Northern Ireland has a very intractable problem of a million unionists who are not to be budged.

Now the reason I call the Ulster Covenant a delinquent act is because if Carson believed that he had to defy a parliamentary majority in Westminster, he was actually defying the constitution of the United Kingdom. Then he should have had the courage to go the distance. It was a treasonous act, the Covenant, by the way. If Carson was going to go for treason, then he should have had the courage of his convictions and gone for independence. He should have gone for UDI like Ian Smith, because that was the logic of his position.

I'm not one of these people who share any admiration for Carson. I had admiration for Craig, who I thought was a pragmatist, but I thought Carson was very like Pearse in the kind of delusionary rhetoric he engaged in. For example, he admitted years later that they should have accepted the first Gladstone Home Rule Bill. He wasn't a partitionist, he mourned the fact that the country was divided; he knew it was an appalling settlement to end up with an appalling 40 per cent Roman Catholic minority. This was no basis for a permanent and stable state. So he knew it in later life and he acted in bad faith in 1912. He fundamentally brought people out in what was the first act in a war of independence to set up a sovereign state of some sort, and hadn't the guts to carry it through. He wanted the best of both worlds. That dichotomy – the dialectic between a quasi-constitutional position on the part of unionism, married to this extreme kind of pro-union rhetoric – was a total contradiction. There's a whole tradition in unionism that at one and the same time is radical and resistant – it's Calvinist republicanism. It's anti-the United Kingdom, anti-being told to do anything, and not really accepting of the rule of law and the monarch. And then that's matched with an excessive rhetoric on behalf of the monarchy. I think unionism has never worked this out for itself intellectually and it needs to do so.

So I don't know how the Covenant centenary will be presented. I think what happened was that Wolfe Tone had a very benign and generally pluralist view of how republicanism would go but it was deeply distorted by a Unitarian, John Mitchel. It was John Mitchel who brought this very vicious physical force and almost hysterical sectarian edge into it, even though he was a Unitarian and from the Protestant tradition. He brought a kind of Calvinism into republicanism – all this, 'If I could grasp the flames of hell in my hand and hurl them in the face of my country's enemies' – and then he went off to become a slaver in the southern states. I regard Mitchel as a very inauthentic person. I was very sorry that Pearse took up that kind of republicanism, which was delusionary and abstract compared to Wolfe Tone's republicanism. Pearse was in a big tradition of European romanticism at the time, like a whole kind of fevered, delusionary nationalism. That somehow you could have an insurrection in Dublin and somehow the Orangemen would join it or help you. Then to think he could take German aid and there'd be no consequences to it. I regard the whole of 1916 as a very delinquent act. Mary McAleese says the men of 1916 were heroes. Well then, what does that make members of the Dublin Metropolitan Police? Ordinary lads from working-class districts who joined the police and suddenly someone comes up and shoots them in the head.

I think 1916 is very problematic and the legacy is particularly problematic – the legacy of 1916 in the Republic. In 1921, we signed the Treaty. Fine, if we signed the Treaty and let it go at that, and ran our state. But we engaged in this rhetoric, leading northern nationalists to believe that somehow we were going to do something for them if they did something. And when they did something, we didn't do anything for them. I think the Republic, the Free State, right up to the rhetoric of the 1966 anniversary, which I remember being on RTÉ at the time, is a very inauthentic tradition. And I think the Republic has no right to parade troops past the GPO without accepting that it's a very problematical tradition, that first of all it was a putsch, it was an attempted coup. Pearse and the others didn't have the support of the public. They got it retrospectively, but at the time, democratically, it was a coup. I have never found any logical or rational way to extol and hail the 1916 men and condemn any other group of republicans that followed them into a coup.

One of the candidates in the presidential election, who suffered at the hands of Martin McGuinness on the famous *Frontline* programme, Sean Gallagher, said at one stage he hoped it wasn't all going to be military pomp and ceremony, although he didn't follow up on that. If Enda Kenny proposes to march the Irish Army past the GPO and to go into the whole 1916 rhetoric, then he should not be surprised if young men who are coming up to sixteen or seventeen years of age start pondering introspectively things like Ireland, united Ireland, nationalism, Pearse and all the boys, what were they fighting for, whatever. Where is all this going to go?

I don't think that happened in 1966 but I think that was an accident of history. In 1966, we were going through a huge revolution. I call it the 'American revolution'. It was a huge sexual and political revolution. There was a big sexual revolution going on, about the Church and about contraception and divorce, and the American civil rights movement rolled over it. And we were coming out of a recession, so there was money around.

The dramas of 1916 depicted in 1966 may have marginally affected young people, but not so much in the Republic of Ireland. I think centenaries generally are very problematical. I remember my grandfather telling me that the 1798 commemoration was the one that brought him into the movement. He joined the IRB, he helped to put up a statue on the Grand Parade, he was on the committee, and from the committee he met members of the IRB and they swore him in. From there he joined the Irish Volunteers. He said that the 1798 commemorations radicalised the young men of Cork.

One hope is that the peace process will be bedded down a bit better by 2016, but I would question any military display by the Republic, with Enda Kenny taking ownership of not just 1916 but what I call the cult of Michael Collins, whereby Fine Gael, which is fundamentally a peaceful constitutional party, takes an inordinate and inappropriate interest in Collins the gunman. They're quite prepared to celebrate Collins on Bloody Sunday shooting a lot of British agents in the head, but I doubt if they would publicly endorse any other group of the IRA shooting anybody in the head in any other part of the island. There's a fundamental hypocrisy and contradiction built into the Republic in its position on 1916.

How should those events be commemorated? I've been thinking about that a lot and the passions that might be inflamed by certain kinds of marching, certain kinds of commemoration. I think there's a great need for the Northern Assembly and the Dáil to get together and set up a kind of parliamentary body that would do its best to influence how both 1912 and 1916 would be commemorated. Now nobody's saying that would be easy, but I regard the Ulster Covenant and 1916 as being twin foundation acts. It's not quite the same thing with the Ulster Covenant, because there's not going to be a British Government endorsing that celebration, but obviously the majority unionist tradition will want to endorse it in some way. I think the time has come to get together a parliamentary body to consider how this whole thing is to be dealt with. The Somme has to be dealt with as part of it, because for me the Somme, despite the horror of it, represents a somewhat benign tradition, a chance to actually talk and bring the two traditions together, because of the common sufferings.

It was absolutely disgraceful, the way the south suppressed the issue, up until recently when the Queen of England visited Islandbridge. I was with a lot of old veterans from the Second World War, from all over Ireland, and they were telling me appalling stories of trying to celebrate. A couple of men in Sligo town were not able to get the FCA to parade to do the military honours because Fianna Fáil or Willie O'Dea or the Ministry of Defence was afraid it might reflect badly on him. There's a lot of foot dragging goes on in these things.

But to go back to 1912, I think we need an all-party parliamentary committee to look at how to commemorate that whole period, to consider it almost as one period of events and to look at the totality. And in looking at the totality, I think you're talking almost entirely about television. It's the only medium that actually has the power to deal with this. That means that BBC Northern Ireland and RTÉ should actually be instructed – I mean it'd not be a matter of freedom – by the parliaments of both states on how to go about the commemoration. They can do their own thing separate from that, but there should be a minimum that both parliaments insist upon. Now this would take some working up, but we've the time to do it.

For example, they need to show programmes that show the problematical side of 1912. In other words, an appropriate unionist producer should be able to do his bit. If the DUP or the UUP want to make a programme about how wonderful it all was, they should be given the facilities to do it, and expert teams. Then someone from an alternative tradition, who doesn't agree with that, who believes, like me, that it was a delinquent act that was full of problems – like why Carson didn't follow through, why he was going around saying he should have accepted the first Home Rule Bill, why in later life he regretted that he'd set up a state with a 40 per cent Catholic minority, which was inherently unstable – needs to make a documentary showing that point of view. I'd like to see a lot of deliberately antagonistic programmes, being transmitted simultaneously by BBC, UTV and the Republic's television – and they should be pretty well simultaneous transmissions, so people would have to turn over to Sky to get away from it! [*Laughs*] I mean that the period would be block-booked for a week or so – a week of commemorations – and you'd have films on 1912 and you'd have films on 1916. Unionists should be invited to make a film on 1916 from their perspective. Northern nationalists or a nationalist grouping should be allowed to make a film showing how they saw 1916-21 as an act of betrayal, almost, of their tradition, with what happened with the Boundary Commission. They should be allowed to put their point of view across. And the Republic should be able to make its constitutional Michael Collins case. In other words, I'd like to see a series where there'd be alternative viewpoints; beautifully produced to the highest production values and with plenty of money spent on it. That's one element of what I call the commemorations.

The second thing I'd like to see done between Northern Ireland and the Republic is something like Pierre Trudeau's Immersion in French course in Canada, where people had to learn French. I think there should be immersion courses, the equivalent of the Coláistí Samhraidh, the summer courses colleges in Ireland, whereby people from the unionist tradition, northern unionists, would be encouraged to come down, or send their sons and daughters down, for an immersion course of six months to a year, which would be properly funded and have a proper reward system, like college subsistence, etc., attached to it, at a university of their choice. I'd like to see a hundred to two hundred northern students in the Republic doing Irish Studies courses in an immersion, living with Irish families, and the reverse happening in Northern Ireland.

Education is a boring word but education is key to this. I'm talking about education – mass education – with these television documentaries. I'm talking about education at the primary-school level, that there be these exchanges in what I call 'Irish Studies Immersion Courses'. Sending an Irish family up to live in the Glens of Antrim, to live the ordinary lives of people and hear the traditions of Orangeism, attend their local Orange hall, listen to unionist historians and northern Protestant historians putting their point of view. You'd want to send a group of them, so they wouldn't feel isolated or that they were being brainwashed, but this immersion in Irish Studies – in the broadest sense of Irish Studies, which includes the northern tradition as well – I'd like to see that go on.

And the third thing I'd like to see is the beginning of mass travel. This has got nothing to do with the unionists at all; it's equally true of northern nationalists – I'd like to see more travel between Northern Ireland and the Republic, and vice versa. Therefore I'd like to see heavily subsidised holidays at a mass level, in which a couple of thousand people a year could take a holiday in Larne or take a holiday in the Glens of Antrim. And that people from the Shankill would be able to come down and have a decent holiday in rural Ireland, in an environment where there's a group of them, and everything would be laid on properly for them. If we designated a year for it, that sort of stuff would go on throughout the entire year.

I think that once you open a mind a little bit, there's no stopping it. I think change is inevitable. I always like to quote John Bruton: he gave a lecture and said that the nationalist tradition in the Republic should have opened itself more fully, opened its eyes to the reality of the unionist presence on the island; but likewise the unionists had an obligation to ask themselves, throughout the Troubles and before, if the Republic weren't better friends of theirs, in many ways, than Britain? To put it brutally, what he implied was that all the British governments, fundamentally regard Dean Swift and the Irish Protestants in the eighteenth century, as the hunchbacks of the tower – a nuisance to be kept quiet, to be thrown a few baubles. He said unionism should reflect how many friends they had in the Irish Republic, both in government, in terms of its actions, and in people like Conor Cruise O'Brien and others – poets and writers – who upheld their democratic rights. 'Would they not reflect on this?' he said. I strongly believe that locking the unionist and nationalist traditions into this cockpit in Northern Ireland – it's like a cauldron. Despite the merits of the peace process and of the Good Friday Agreement, there's been no shift in sectarianism, no real shift. This is what preoccupies me. I'm always abused for being revisionist and anti-nationalist, but I think I take a deeper interest. I read all the papers in Northern Ireland, and it seems to me not much has changed. I mean there's the surface patina, but fundamentally the old tribal animosities are there.

I believe what is needed is a third force almost, where Northern nationalists can get away from their aggro with the unionists and their aggro with the south. We need to open up, so that unionists don't feel pressurised, that they don't have to deal with nationalists, that they have a few friends down here. That would ease out the situation. There'd be a number of people like me down here who'd be very anxious to secure the rights of unionists in any federal situation. And that's what I'm talking about. I believe that, ultimately, what we have to work towards is a federal parliament. We need an arrangement of de Valera's Document No. 2. It's very unfashionable to say so, but it was a very ingenious document. Two circles, one inside the other. I believe that we should have an all-island federal Ireland within one circle, with the two parliaments within one circle, sending representatives to an all-Ireland parliament, and that it should be within an All-Ireland–Commonwealth arrangement. It would allay the fears of unionists. But on such a small island, it is ridiculous to have two parliaments functioning. We should be working the situation where we allow them to wither away, both Stormont and the Dáil, and let a federal parliament do the business of the day. The unionists need have no fear because the protocols of the Good Friday Agreement are still there, if they wish to apply them. And I believe it could work, and very quickly – even in my lifetime. I believe in ten years of federal arrangements and travel between the two, nationalists would realise okay, they've got friends in the south but not all of them are friends of theirs, and unionists would realise they've got enemies in the south but not all are enemies there – these relationships would come out in a federal parliament. And that's what Conor Cruise O'Brien was at, at the end of his life. It was an extraordinary journey. At the end of his life he returned to where he'd started. He believed unionists were safer in an Irish Parliament than they would ever be with a British Parliament, because fundamentally he didn't believe that the British were honest brokers.

I was in the Reform Group for a while that was pushing the Commonwealth return idea, but I left it because I knew it was not important. Although it's very interesting that Éamon Ó Cuív of Fianna Fáil has no problems with the Commonwealth; Fianna Fáil doesn't have huge problems with the Commonwealth. The Commonwealth is a kind of a non-body; I don't know how much interest unionists would have in that. I was thinking of something more substantial than the Commonwealth, I was thinking of doing the old Arthur Griffith dual monarchy Sinn Féin thing, where the Queen was given some kind of titular representation in the wider scheme of things. The inner circle would be the Irish Parliament, which is effectively an all-Ireland parliament, and to me is as close as we're going to get to a united Ireland – in the next twenty or thirty years anyway. And that should be within some wider constitutional arrangement, to relax unionists, number one, but also to give the south that dimension we got during the Queen's visit, showing the British identity in the south and people who fought in the British Army. In a wider circle outside of that, the Queen and the President, Uachtarán na hÉireann, should be equal partners; there'd be no *primus inter pares*. So there would be two dignitaries at the top of de Valera's outer circle, and that circle would be the parliament. That's something I've been thinking about for a long time as an interim solution on the way to a united Ireland.

Timing of media events is a huge problem and I think that the 2012 boat has been missed there. I was hoping that it could be brought in retrospectively to the Larne gun-running of 1914; that we'd aim for 1914, plus the Somme, plus 1916 as a kind of triad. And in relation to the Larne gun-running, I imagined units of the Irish Army and units of the British Army, and voluntary bodies from the north, forming kind of a corps; a commemorative corps which would march to Larne and march to Howth, and attend the re-enactment, with dignitaries from both states present. Military honours would be afforded at Larne by elements of the Irish Army (now to get them across the border would be a day's work), but there would also be elements of the British Army present to commemorate Erskine Childers' gun-running.

For the Somme, I'd like to see a long march to Tipperary. They say it's a long way to Tipperary; I'd like to see a march of a unit, a combined, composite unit, with the British Army, Irish Army and other organised elements, from Boy Scouts, for example. We could think about things like the Fianna, if there's [*Laughs*], if there's no dimension of subversion about it ... but there may be bodies that want to march – Orange bands, Hibernian bands, etc. I think there's a very good case for doing a march from Larne to Tipperary, a march from Dublin to Tipperary, and a march from Howth to Tipperary, converging on Tipperary town, for 1916. Units would march from all over Ireland to represent the Ulster Division and the Southern Division at the Somme. Let that be a week-long celebration, with trains again subsidised. I remember watching guys from the north – Northern Ireland unionists who didn't identify themselves as such (there's a lot of them come down to the Republic and don't say they are) – at the Connaught Rangers museum, fascinated by it. I had relations that soldiered with them. Tipperary has great museums in relation to the First World War. I think you need imaginative enterprises like the 'Long Way to Tipperary March'. The 1916 celebration at the GPO – nothing will stop the Irish Government trying to take ownership of that. They're going to do their military parades. I think it's very important that there's a big representation of Northern Ireland there – from both communities.

One of the crucial things, I believe, is that there must be a committee of historians north and south set up, representative of republican, nationalist and unionist traditions, to devise a week of lectures and commemorations; well-attended and televised lectures, with serious arguments: about what happened between '16 and '21; about the Border Commission; about what happened to northern nationalists; about what happened to northern unionists; about whether the Republic has clean hands. I'd like to see serious debates on primetime television all through that week.

I actually think it can be done. For example, if you can get the beginning of a debate going in Stormont between the traditions and something like the Oireachtas committees – an all-party committee – to study what should be done about the Somme, 1916, the Larne gun-running, accepting that they've lost the 1912 one. I think the existence of that committee and its expressed desire to see televised public events, serious historical lectures, and imaginative events, would put enormous pressure on the Republic to adjust the way it goes about that.

The SDLP and Sinn Féin might flatly say, for example, 'We think there are a lot of problems about the way you intend to celebrate this. There's nothing we have to celebrate about the Treaty of 1921; that wasn't a particularly happy time for us.' That's a whole dimension that's left out of the Republic's celebration, which goes, 'All our history came out of 1916, then there was the Treaty, then there was Michael Collins, he was shot, and that's the end.' It's kind of 'happy days' and 'we got a Republic.' That was the beginning of a hard time for northern nationalists and that problem has to be integrated into any arrangement. It's not just 1916; we're talking about the whole prospectus and that period. Northern nationalists' grievances, historical grievances, have to be reflected.

Then there are the unionists' grievances. I think there are unionist grievances about the way the Republic never took them seriously or understood them; I think they have grievances that nationalists never understood or took seriously. I even think there are elements within the unionists that have grievances with the British Government. There's a brand of historical unionist – I'm just thinking that my friend Roy Garland would have a lot of problems with elements of the Ulster establishment – the Paisleys, the DUP, the Craigs, the O'Neills, who misled the working class, and so the whole aspect of unionists being used as cannon fodder has to be brought out. In other words, historians and television will have the crucial part to play in this, rather than armies or bands.

I don't think we're going to have a simple military ceremony in Dublin. Northern republicans, beginning with Alex Maskey some years back, have been quite good about paying tribute and honouring the important sacred moments of unionism. I confidently expect to see Sinn Féin members of the Northern Assembly at these unionist ceremonies. I would also expect to see representatives of unionism at the GPO in Dublin. I certainly would hope so. I mean not just hoping, to be honest; there should be *coercive insistence* that this happens, because not to do so is hardly within the spirit of the Good Friday Agreement and all the rest of it.

But will it be done? I actually think there's going to be quite a lively debate opened up in the Republic about 1916. I read Kevin Myers this morning in the *Irish Independent*. He said, 'The centenaries are upon us. What are we doing about them? How are we going to handle them?', and he went through the Larne gun-running, the whole lot. Now, I don't think it's a very deep article, and he hasn't really thought about it profoundly, he just identifies that it's going to be problematical – and it is going to be problematical. Therefore I think the sooner a parliamentary body is set up the better, and I think the SDLP and Sinn Féin should take the initiative on this. I mean jointly take the initiative and approach their unionist counterparts and say, 'What about us in all this? I mean they're going to be doing 1916 in Dublin, what about the Somme, what about the Ulster Covenant? The unionist side want to celebrate this; it's problematical for us. What about the whole lot? What about the Boundary Commission, what about Carson?'

Even a public debate on Carson's politics would be fascinating. He thought the settlement of 1921 was a total disaster; he did not want it. That opens up huge questions, like why did the Republic ignore all the simmering problems there from 1921 until it broke up in their faces? And then wring their hands but come up with nothing credible? The reaction was always so slow from the Republic, although it was not slow with everyone at the top. Lemass was continually aware that Northern Ireland was a constant problem. He saw it as a double problem: the problem of the Catholic minority and the problem of the Republic's failure to understand Northern Ireland Protestants or Northern Ireland Catholics. The other day I came across some very interesting stuff about Lemass and Patrick McGilligan, who was the secretary of the Department of Finance in the Inter-party government of 1948. He strongly believed that Ireland should rejoin the Commonwealth as an act of appeasement to northern unionism, in order to open up talks that would ease into a discussion of where we all were. And he was shot down – nobody wanted to join.

But it shows that there was thinking going on. Whittaker, of course, was the shrewdest of all. Whittaker knew that any adventurism by Haughey had no military ordinance or numbers to back it up in 1970 – they were just posturing. Whittaker knew the strength of the Irish Army and its training levels.

I know there's a large consensus of political wisdom to let sleeping dogs lie. Fundamentally, it strikes me that the majority of southern opinion – I'm not too sure about northern opinion, or if there's a consensus – is that we've got the Good Friday Agreement and everything's fine. I regard the sectarian problem as a ticking time bomb. It's always there and it's there to be exploited by any generation. So I've always feared things that stand still. I believe that stasis builds up serious discontents like a head of steam. It would be very wrong if you were to treat the Good Friday Agreement as the equivalent of the Boundary Commission, and just let things sit for another forty years. Delving into our past is always dangerous, but it is actually safer to go towards the nettle and grasp it – you get stung less. It would be far better if we went forward.

Let's have a look at the Larne gun-running, let's have a look at what it means. Was it actually a noble and heroic act? Or was it a delinquent act, whereby you're defying the parliament of the United Kingdom and then haven't the guts to follow it through? Let's look at 1916. Was it a coup? Did it have popular support? If it didn't have popular support and it got retrospective support, what's to prevent any other group of republicans making the same argument, and how can we put them outside the fold without giving them a logical argument? It seems to me that if you want peace in Ireland you'd have to condemn the Larne gun-running. Unionism would have to say it was a load of shit, the whole thing was wrong; nationalism would have to say that if we buy into 1916, we can't really argue against the Provisional IRA or any other IRA. And we'd have to stop and start afresh.

The Somme, as I said, offers the benign interpretation. I would like to see Frank McGuinness's great play *Observe the Sons of Ulster.* I'd like to see a lot of other plays commissioned, and films. I do think we have to get to grips with television somehow, so that it's not swanning off and dismissing everybody with a debate on *Spotlight* on the Larne gun-running. I think we should dedicate a week of commemorations. Not necessarily in 2014; 2016 might actually be quite a good year, because the Somme was in 1916, and it's within kicking distance of '14. That year, 2015/6, could be a year in which Northern Ireland and the Republic delve dispassionately and with open eyes into their respective histories. And let the chips fall. It fundamentally would be a campaign of mass public education in which none of the three traditions on the island – northern nationalism, northern unionism or republican constitutional nationalism – would come out with clean hands.

DANNY MORRISON

Danny Morrison is an Irish republican writer and former press officer of Sinn Féin. He is also the secretary of the Bobby Sands Trust and current chairman of Féile an Phobail.

Background

My father's family would not have been republican, and not that pro-nationalist either. Somewhere along the line there are Protestants, because Morrison is a Scottish Presbyterian name. My Granda Morrison fought in the First World War, in the Royal Flying Corps. Then he came out of the war, and was arrested in Currie Street Hall and charged with raising funds for the IRA. He defended himself and he got off, because, he explained, 'How could I be doing this? I've just been demobbed from the Royal Flying Corps.' Then he went down south and joined the Free State Army for a while, deserted and came back to the north. When the Second World War broke out, he joined the RAF again and was based in Malta. Towards the end of the Second World War my father joined the RAF but mostly as a painter of planes, rather than as a combatant.

On my mother's side, my grandparents, the Whites, had been burnt out of two houses in the 1920s and '30s. Finally they moved to Andersonstown, which was just being built at that stage. My uncle Harry – my mother's older brother – was in jail two or three times and on the last occasion he was sentenced to death for the killing of a Special Branch man in Dublin, for which his comrade had already been arrested and executed by firing squad.

My other uncle, who was married to my mother's eldest sister, was a Stormont MP for a while in the late 1940s. He was republican Labour for the Docks area.

My radicalisation came in stages. In 1966 there was the Easter Rising fiftieth anniversary commemorations; that was a huge event. There were republicans who had been in jail in the 1940s; my Uncle Harry came up to see his old friends, people like Billy McKee and Prionsas McArt. My uncle Seamus and my uncle George played in céilí bands – in the White family there was a big tradition of Irish music. The Felons' Club also opened around 1966 or '67, which was an illegal shebeen; the pageantry of it, the colour of it impressed me. At school I was picked to play a very small part as a Russian peasant in an Irish language play and we eventually made it through to the Gate Theatre in Dublin. In 1966, the same year as the fiftieth anniversary of the Easter Rising, we won the all-Ireland competition for this Irish language drama.

That deepened the nationalism I already had. Plus we were poor. We couldn't afford to go away on summer holidays. So what happened every summer in the late 1950s, and every summer up to about '63 or '64, was that my uncle Harry, who lived in Dublin and was married to a Kerry woman – this is the man who'd been in jail several times, who had been sentenced to death – would go on his holidays to Kerry and we would go from Belfast to his house in Dublin. So we were aware that Dublin was the capital of Ireland, we saw the GPO, we were taken to places like Nelson's Pillar, which was still standing – I think it was blown up in '66 – although we never went up it, maybe because we were conscious it was named after Nelson. Also in the late '60s, my uncle Harry and his wife Kathleen were on the committee to restore Kilmainham Gaol.

So there were all these small influences. But to me the biggest influence came from the street: what you saw, what you witnessed, what you heard. The big Easter commemoration came up the Falls Road, and people were pointed out to you, 'Oh, you see him? He got the cat o' nine tails in the '40s!', and, 'He escaped from Derry jail!' We looked at these figures with awe. Nobody ridiculed them. Although they may have been held by some to be eccentric or to be a minority, they were invested with a lot of respect – sort of venerated.

Then, just after '66, the Felons' Club was opened in the old boys' home in the abandoned mill down in Milltown Road. I was asked to come down and make sandwiches and tea when they were having functions. I was mixing with these people but there was no debate. They had their little intimate language which they used to among themselves. I was just thirteen or fourteen years of age.

I lived in Iveagh Parade and across the road from us lived Peter Ward. He was a young barman who worked in the International Hotel. He was lured to Malvern Street where he was killed by the UVF, which had been reorganised under the leadership of Gusty Spence and several others. He was buried in Beechmount, in our area. Later, when I got married in 1974, eight years after this event, his mother was a close neighbour of mine. We saw his funeral and in our eyes it was almost loyalist revenge because we had commemorated Easter 1916.

Then there was the scandal of John Scullion, who was walking up Clonard Street when he was shot. The RUC said he was stabbed and the family said he was shot. His body was exhumed and the cops were embarrassed when it was revealed that they'd covered up the fact that he'd been shot, and it was the same UVF gang who'd killed him. We believed that we were being punished for expressing our nationalism.

The Centenaries

The plans for commemoration of the signing of the Covenant are already afoot. In fact, I think City Hall has controversially set aside some millions for that.

The nationalist community has a much more mature attitude towards unionists celebrating their history than unionists have toward nationalists celebrating their history. That was because unionists, for fifty or sixty years, were led to believe that they were superior to nationalists. They were going to smash Sinn Féin and now they're in government with the IRA (I use that term ironically), so after a long, long time we have a power-sharing administration. But unionists have come round in many respects to realising that the game is up.

The unionists have cornered the market on the First World War and the Somme. Yet the fact is that 55,000 people from the Irish Volunteers – the nationalist tradition – died, having been sold the pup that they were fighting for small nations. The Home Rule Bill, they were told, postponed at the start of the First World War, would be enacted at the end of it.

Let's deal with the centenary of 1912 first of all. When you commemorate such an event, it requires reflection on why your grandparents or your great-grandparents did what they did, and whether or not it stands up to historical scrutiny. I think that any unionist who is honest could not, hand on heart, say that the whole history of the Covenant was in the best interests of even their community. The UVF was the first paramilitary army of the twentieth century. Bonar Law encouraged illegality; Edward Carson did exactly the same. Prior to the setting up of the UVF, Catholics were driven out of the shipyard in July 1912.

It's okay having these commemorations but it's through their current circumstances that people will mediate this back-memory. Obviously unionists will go through the motions, they will probably have pageants. Whether they will be as prepared as we have been to discuss and debate, revise and analyse, is another thing.

I don't think it's going to lead to the current political situation being rolled back in any way. Whether or not unionists believe that the commitment of those who signed the Ulster Covenant has been maintained, they're certainly going to claim it. Although I doubt if they'll believe it, because those who signed in their own blood, they signed a Covenant for the nine counties to remain outside the third proposed Home Rule legislation. So they actually ditched their brethren in Cavan, Monaghan and Donegal, basically for sectarian reasons, because they wanted to have the largest amount of land mass that the numbers gave them.

Similarly, the things the men of 1916 died for have not been realised. They declared a republic. That proclamation had certain social and economic values attached to it that we can say were socialist or left-wing or radical. They certainly weren't conservative. They spoke about cherishing all of the children equally, which is taken to include the unionists. They didn't answer the fact that Redmond had earlier agreed to the exclusion of six counties on a temporary basis. It was never discussed for how long. The point I'm making is that no republican can be satisfied while there is a link with Britain. That's it, simply put. So there is unfinished business.

We need to think about how we diminish that link and move through a process of transition, embracing everyone on this island, making sure you don't trigger a panic reaction in the unionist community, making sure that everybody is transparent about what their objectives are, what their motives are. The process we currently have, while imperfect, means people like myself, who've been in jail and who've taken part in armed struggle for freedom, can look to the future. I think that history is not on the unionist side and I think that they feel that. I have seen more and more unionists describe themselves as Northern Irish. Of course pure Irish people say, 'Oh no, they shouldn't be; they're pure Irish, they shouldn't be using that term "Northern Irish".' I don't have any objection to it because I think it's a shift in thinking. It means they're thinking more about here, rather than over there – the British connection. And most of them know anyway, when they go to London, they're considered to be Paddies.

There is, of course, the fact that a majority of people in the north must vote for constitutional change. And we've got another problem: there needs to be a majority in the south of Ireland as well. Besides which, if we're going to be realistic, a united Ireland – even though for romantic reasons and for aspirational reasons I want to see it – has to make social, economic and political sense. Those, therefore, are the three goals we have to be working towards.

That said, over the last thirty years the whole notion of sovereignty has undergone considerable change. When you consider what's happening in Europe, when you even consider the euro, the currency which is common to so many countries in the European Union, there's a notion of pooled sovereignty now. People have lost rights because they've agreed it's for the greater good. Although it's debatable who benefits the most: the entrepreneurs, the capitalists, the industrialists, the financiers, or the people on the ground?

I still consider myself to be a nationalist. I was in England recently at a wedding. The number of St George's flags that were up in England! It's as if there's a resurgence of English nationalism because of devolution to Scotland.

The 1916 ideal of sovereignty is not beside the point now, because the germ of what they were talking about was people's rights and national rights. We tried to get our civil rights and we discovered that we couldn't get them. And so our civil rights were linked to getting our nationalist rights and the degree of oppression justified the armed struggle here. Now, we've got a halfway house, because the British Government has recognised the republican struggle, prisoners have been amnestied, Sinn Féin's arguments have been endorsed to the extent that Sinn Féin have dramatically overtaken the SDLP, and in all likelihood you might have a former IRA leader becoming First Minister in the North of Ireland. Now that is an incredible story. Contrast that with the Palestinians. Every time they struggle they end up losing more territory. But here we have a template which I believe has worked, at a cost. It could have been avoided, but for it to have been avoided, the unionists would have had to adapt to accepting our rights. In fact, what you could foresee now is those two polities slowly move towards each other, which is why I talk about this harmonisation as people get relaxed.

Here is a small example. My brother and I were camping down in Galway. He had just been released from the H-Blocks; he'd been sentenced to twenty-six years in jail and got out under the Good Friday Agreement. We were in this camp in Salthill near Galway, and this guy drives in in a Jeep, gets out and goes over to his tent. My brother said,

'He was in the H-Blocks! He's a fucking screw!' I said, 'Are you sure?' So I went over to the guy and he turned white. The first thing he said to me was, 'I was never a beater. I never beat any prisoners.' Then my brother said, 'Come on over here, have a beer.' We got him relaxed. He was from Newtownards and he was saying, 'You know, I think this is my country as well.' We said, 'It *is* your country. It is your country.' Then he said, 'We were just leaving', and I replied, 'No you weren't. You weren't leaving.' And he says, 'Okay, I wasn't leaving.' [*Laughs*] He had a couple of beers with us, and later his kid came over and lent us a pump for our air bed.

The point I'm making is, in the current situation people will start to think outside of the traditional box. For example, I don't think there's anybody believes the twenty-six counties should come into the Commonwealth. I don't think that's a runner. But I do believe there are unionists who are thinking that the original reasons for opposing and breaking up the nation don't hold today. The basic argument could be that we get money from Westminster and they owe us, because we were great during the Second World War and during the First World War (although in fact, again, probably more people from the south fought in the Second World War than unionists from the north).

But I think there is an openness developing. I see my role as chair of Féile an Phobail as holding out the hand of friendship and trying to encourage this at a local level, across the Shankill and Sandy Row, and the Village area – building up contacts and using culture and arts for that purpose. When I say history is on our side, I think that economically it is madness to have a hospital here and a hospital there, and both crippling the separate economies. There's a need for a pooling of resources. It's madness to have different agricultural policies, different fishing policies, different tourism policies. I don't see any reason why, at some stage, the unionists who start calling themselves Northern Irish can't be convinced, provided it makes the case that a new configuration on this island will come into being with their support.

The law is, there has to be a majority of the community in the north. That is the law and the unionists cannot get round it. Now what if a plague comes down on the north and somehow only wipes out 500,000 Protestants? Suddenly nationalists find themselves in the majority. Of course legally, constitutionally, nationalists could trigger a referendum that'd deliver a united Ireland. Whether or not that's the wisest thing to do is something that could only be decided in the circumstances.

If a large number of unionists then felt that they were able to ratchet up the tempo – that now *we're* being oppressed, now *we're* being forced in here; now they're going to do (although they wouldn't say this) what we did to them – you could end up with bloodshed on a scale that would spoil it. So there are grounds for thinking the gracious thing might be the best thing. It's not in my power, by the way, it's just a single opinion that one person holds, a person who has been through it and who argued all his life against the unionist veto on TV, radio, in elections, and in an armed struggle … I'm getting old [*Laughs*].

As the time of a nationalist majority approaches, and provided everybody is level with each other, it may well be the case that significant figures in the unionist community – writers or clerics or even politicians – will say, 'Well folks, those were the rules that were established, so we have to play according to the rules, or else the world could turn against us; we could lose public opinion.' And Britain, by the way, could be pulled over the coals internationally if the agreement wasn't honoured, so you could do it.

But I think there is much more to be gained from knowing you could do it and not doing it at that point in time. In their speeches in the run-up to Easter 2016, republicans should be saying to unionists that we're welcoming them to a new Ireland, a united Ireland. Back then, these were the circumstances and here's why they took the stance they did. Things have changed; we inherited the outcome of that period.

The template that we have for the 1916 centenary is the re-interment of 1916 men like Kevin Barry in Glasnevin Cemetery about four or five years ago, maybe longer. I wrote a piece about it, in which a journalist – was it Fintan O'Toole or Henry McDonald, or maybe Eoghan Harris? – asked, 'What's this for, why are we doing this now?' But the streets of Dublin were bunged ten deep on the road up to Glasnevin from Dublin. So a spirit of freedom still exists in the Irish people. There's a whole lot of people who're going to be vying to claim 1916: Ruairí Ó Brádaigh will be saying he owns it, Fianna Fáil are going to be saying they own it, and Sinn Féin are going to be saying, well, it's everybody's. I hope that's the message. Fine Gael are going to be saying, 'Actually it was our people went out, because Garret Fitzgerald's father was in the GPO' – all of this, instead of looking at it historically. If you feel passionate or romantic or emotional about it, express it whatever way you wish. But it should not be exploited or used as a hammer to hurt or to put down anyone, or to prove a current political point.

ENDA KENNY

Enda Kenny is the leader of Fine Gael and Taoiseach of the Republic of Ireland. He served as Minister for Tourism and Trade from 1994 to 1997. He is the longest-serving TD currently in Dáil Éireann.

Background

From the time I was a young child, politics was central to our household. My father was a deputy for the old Mayo West constituency and the old South Mayo constituency. That was from 1954, when I was three, up until 1975, when he died, after which I was elected myself. So politics was in the genes, you could say.

You observe it as a child in a political household and you gain an innate understanding of what makes people tick, how you should treat people and the political issues of the day. So while it would never have been discussed in the context of one party versus another, by observation and understanding you begin to get an insight into the fears and the pressures on politicians, but also the way they conducted their business with people. My late mother didn't talk politics that much but her attendance at political functions here and there gave you an understanding of what was going on and why it was necessary to attend some of these things. And of course in my childhood years, you observed the run-up to elections and election campaigns; the way they were fought then as opposed to the way they are fought now. So you understand all that too.

Most people do inherit their politics from their family, unless they rebel and go off in a different direction entirely. If you get involved in political campaigns, you begin to understand the issues. So in my time, and likewise with most of the people from the different parties I would have known over those years, they learned their politics in the same way and in most cases continued on. Not in every case however; there were some exceptions would have gone the other way, would have joined different parties – or given up entirely [*Laughs*]. But by and large you follow on, and because you are involved from one side or the other, you begin to delve into the issues and the principles of what the party stands for, and see how that is implemented.

Time has not so much changed as confirmed for me that politics is first and last about people. It's about their lives, about their opportunities, about their careers. Good politics for me is to give everybody equal opportunity to make their way. That's been solidified and reinforced by what I've seen, by what I was able to put into practice as a Dáil deputy or as a minister in the previous government. But now, as Taoiseach, you can see the imprimatur of using the lever of government in the people's interests and in the country's interests. That really is what appeals to me. It's a challenge every day, every minute – but enjoyable too. The privilege of holding this office is one that comes to few politicians, and therefore I appreciate it completely, with a sense of humility. Where I come from [*Laughs*] … as one of the security people said to me in New York last week, when I came out of the room carrying my own bag, he said, 'You know, it's a pity some of the folks in Washington wouldn't do that!' [*Laughs*]

The Centenaries

To come to the Ulster Covenant. It was signed by almost half a million people, men and women; some signed it in blood, and that's an indication of how deeply rooted the feelings were about Ulster and about the threat to Ulster as it was seen then, in being contrary to the Home Rule Bill. While women didn't have the vote at the time, they still had over 200,000 of them sign for the Ulster Covenant. It was a demonstration of the scale and depth of the people saying, 'You can't and you won't touch the province in which we live.'

Yes, the Covenant was contrary to the wishes of the people of Ireland, and you've had cyclical reaction up and down over the years. We're glad to be in the position we're in now, where you've got peace and communities working together in the interests of the island of Ireland, while respecting the different traditions.

We're heading into a decade of commemorations, and there is a huge spectrum of circumstances and events that people might want to commemorate in their own individual way. What I've tried to do here, in working with the British Government and the Northern Ireland people, is to lead on this in a constructive and sensitive fashion. That's why I've set up a committee, under the chairmanship of the Minister for Arts and Heritage and Culture, Jimmy Deenihan, to look at the politics of that, and a panel of professional historians, chaired by Dr Maurice Manning, to look at the accuracy of what should be commemorated, how it should be commemorated, and to put that together over the next couple of years so that we get a comprehensive, sensitive way of doing this. Some parties might want to commemorate them in different ways than others.

You now have so many young historians around, with so much more relevant information coming to light, that clearly there is a huge appetite throughout the country for this kind of information. For instance, I launched a book down in Meath on the war dead of the county who fought in the Great War, and 600 people turned up to that. A number of years ago, down in my own county [Mayo], they converted a piece of waste ground into a beautiful peace park which commemorated not only 1914-18 but every other war in which people from the county fought. I'm astounded at the connections that come from abroad – I see this because the names are etched in stone there. What I'm saying is, you're not going to have a bloc out of this committee saying, 'Well, here is the Covenant, here is 1916, here is the Somme.' You're going to have a spectrum of commemorative events.

But if we look at the Somme commemoration, I think what is going to happen is that the Minister and his group are going to take soundings about this, as will the professional panel, and they will make a recommendation in consultation with everyone else as to what should happen. What I don't want to happen is individual parties trying to use historic events for current-day agendas. You don't want a party's current philosophy hyped up because of the fact that a historic event should be commemorated in a particular way.

We should all be willing to learn why and how these things happened in the first place, and their relevance in the period in which they happened, and what relationship that might have to the world we live in now. So what we're at here really, in addressing this, is being as inclusive as we can and as understanding as we can, so that you're not going to have a free-for-all in respect of particular kinds of commemorations. It's to have an overview of our history and the events that occurred in that history; it's how you refer to those, it's how you consider how they might be commemorated, and how you consider what kind that commemoration should be.

I don't want to take away from any group the historic fact of their origins. I go to the council chamber in Belfast and see the table upon which the Covenant was signed; here is a memento of history with a particular story. So the unionist people will refer to the Covenant as being a foundation of their fundamental beliefs and I have no intention of taking that away from them. What is important is how you refer to that event and the depth of feeling around it, and having an understanding of what it meant then, of how it came about, based on previous covenants or whatever, and its historic significance or implications now.

When these commemorations have ended, I'd like people to be more aware of the country we live in, and the series of historic events that happened that make us the kind of people that we are. I think it would be right and fitting that people, irrespective of their political background, would have a much deeper and clearer understanding of the reasons why these things happened and what it means in the context of our current island and our politics.

As for attendance at Covenant events, I was actually talking to the Minister for Foreign Affairs, who was invited, I think, to one or two events. I don't see any reason why not. Certainly the Minister for Arts who is chairing the committee here would be more than willing to attend. I think that we should reflect on the best way that this should be done. You don't want a situation where Person X attended this, therefore you must attend Y. It's not that kind of tit-for-tat at all. This is an opportunity to look down on the history of both parts of the island and on this series of events and say, 'How has this shaped us as a people? How has it determined what we're doing now as we face a challenging future?' When I talk to First Minister Robinson and Deputy First Minister McGuinness, and see the polarised positions they have come from, as they put a joint programme together in the joint interest of the same province, but as a consequence the peoples north and south, I can see there are opportunities for real progress as a people. So it's a case of looking down on it, not looking back individually and saying well, this was X or Y. It's the evolution of the peoples, the events and circumstances, through all those challenging and different times to where we are now.

Regarding the Easter Rising, again I'd like to see the bringing on of so much more information that's now available about these events. For instance, the military archives which are held in Cathal Brugha Barracks are the most fascinating body of material I think I have ever come across. Hundreds of thousands of files. We're going to release these online over the next few years, which will give people a much deeper understanding of their forefathers and how they got involved in different things, from before 1916 on. So what I want out of it is that all this information will be put out there, so that people can read, understand and think more deeply about what has shaped them.

Comparisons between what the Proclamation hoped for Ireland and the present situation? That's being done now anyway. You'll hear people quoting from sections of the Proclamation to say, 'Have we achieved what was set out here?' But when you read some of the military archives, you see where the leaders of 1916 arranged for their executions and all of the material that's currently not in the public domain. I think it's fascinating material. Of course you're going to have comparisons between aspirations that were set out in that Proclamation and where, ninety years on, we are not in control of our economic sovereignty, to the point where we are in a programme out of which we must emerge and will emerge in the shortest possible time.

The Easter 1916 hope of a thirty-two-county republic – this is the big argument. There isn't any reason why people can't still aspire to that, but the Good Friday Agreement sets out the position very clearly. If, on some future occasion, the peoples north and south decide themselves that this should happen, both governments have already agreed that.

I do think there's a lot to be learned. When I went to school myself, history stopped before John Redmond; if you got as far as the turn of the century at all, that was it. So you went through a blank period in secondary school in my time, where it wasn't actually taught as history at all. Now we're in a very different position. So I'd like to think that with all of the communications and stuff that's available now, that our people, wherever they come from and whatever their beliefs or creeds, are going to have a much deeper understanding of the way that we've been shaped.

Actually we commemorate Easter 1916 annually: there's a state commemoration every Easter Sunday, which is a very short, very dignified, very respectful occasion, and I think it brings its own poignancy and message, standing outside the GPO. You had a different sort of celebration in 1966 [*Laughs*], when they celebrated the fiftieth anniversary of the Rising. Most people living in the country don't remember that at all – they read about it – 1966. But I think it shaped people's opinions between then and now. And the next decade is going to give brilliant opportunity for these celebrations.

But one of the things that I want to ensure doesn't happen is what I said earlier on: you don't want individuals or groups or organisations making a major issue of some particular aspect or circumstance that they want commemorated or highlighted in a particular way. That's why I think that you have to involve all of the political process and the historians with historical accuracy to say, 'This is how we should remember these events or circumstances.' Because while you can have individuals or parties or organisations that may very well hold dearly to an event or circumstance, you don't want it – for want of a better word – hijacked at the expense of the evolution of where we actually are here. That's why I think that you chair this by government but that you reflect the views and the considered opinions of the entire political spectrum, and parallel that with historical accuracy from professional historians. In that way, you're going to get an inclusive, overall concept that will be beneficial for all the people.

I would, of course, welcome debate. And there are going to be quite intense discussions, I'm sure. That will be healthy, provided it stays within reasonable limits. To talk about these historic issues, events and circumstances is always healthy.

As to comparisons between the hopes of those who signed the Proclamation and today, you could take different views from different governments in the intervening period, where they said they'd like to see a different kind of Ireland. I don't want to use clichés here, but the future is the only place we have to live. And I think there's a much clearer sense now of what interdependencies and interconnectedness are. Of all the small countries in the world, we have a unique opportunity to tie these strands together in a global diaspora, in a way that few other countries can match. So I welcome healthy debate about these things. These are historic events and historic issues. It's a time long past, it's an Ireland long gone. We're facing the challenge of a world that is evolving before our very eyes; if we're not prepared to ride the waves of change that are coming, then we lose out. So given all our historic traditions, given all the circumstances that have honed us as a people, I actually feel that we are in a very strong position to continue to make the disproportionate impact that we've made on global politics and global business for the future.

And I don't see why unionists mightn't attend Easter Rising ceremonies. Keeping in mind the fact that the Queen of Great Britain herself came here, the fact that she attended at the Garden of Remembrance, which commemorated those who rebelled and rose and fought and died in risings against the British Empire for centuries; the fact that she attended at Islandbridge and gave recognition to those who followed Redmond's advice and went to fight for king and country, for the freedom of small nations. As I said in College Green: close that circle of history.

We're on a different island now, in a different Ireland now. I think it's useful to be able to reflect on the maturity of our peoples and our parties, and I think that's evident in the way things have moved in the last number of years.

There has been a significant shift in the attitude towards those here who fought in the British Army during the First World War, in what was probably the most wanton slaughter of human beings ever. The fact that no generals in the British Army ever went near the front line and stayed well out of range. The fact that diaries of German gunners would say the barrels of their machine guns were red-hot, with young men of sixteen years and upwards marching to their death. To read about it, and the absolute wanton slaughter of a million in Verdun and at the Somme and at Passchendaele, was quite extraordinary. To also read about people who were destroyed – exited from the forces, taken out by their own and shot for desertion. And the fact that those who survived and came back to Ireland were not recognised for their belief and for what they did. It's time to have that closed off, and I was very glad that President McAleese and Her Majesty the Queen were able to do that and be recognised as such by governments as well.

At that time, you had people involved in the streets of Dublin fighting for the freedom of Ireland and you had their peers fighting in the trenches in the First World War – young men from the same parishes and the same communities. One goes to fight for Irish freedom, one goes to fight for the freedom of small nations. They lost their lives in many cases. Some survived and were treated differently. I think that's because of the political pressures of the time and because of the association with fighting for the British Army. Yet you still have lots of Irishmen in the British forces today – in the RAF and the Navy, and whatever else.

I do see dangers attached to all of these centenaries. You don't want a situation where – for want of a better word again – things are hijacked for a different purpose by organisations or by any party, which is why we want to be as inclusive in this as we can. I recognise, for instance, that the unionist people will want to celebrate the Ulster Covenant or other issues in their own way. Some will want greater emphasis on one circumstance than another. But at the same time, it's important to bear in mind there's been an evolution of time, an evolution of political understanding and an evolution over the period to the kind of people we are now. The overall intent here, in having this decade of commemoration and ceremony, is to have people as fully informed as they can be and to have all of that information made available to them so that they can inform themselves, and feel deep inside themselves that they have a better understanding of who they are, what has formed them, and how these things happened in the first place. I think in a local historic sense as well, you have, as I said, a lot of local information now coming to light that mightn't have been available previously, which will deepen people's understanding of what happened in their area or their community or to their people.

I'm optimistic. You will never find me being a pessimist. As I say, we have to look to the future; it's the only place we have to live in. And as President Clinton used to say, 'Values rooted in tradition are important, but we have to reflect on these things carefully.'

JIM ALLISTER

Jim Allister is a senior barrister and leader of the Traditional Unionist Voice party (TUV), serving as its sole MLA in the Stormont Assembly. He was formerly a member of the DUP and served as an MEP for that party from 2004 to 2009.

Background

I suppose growing up as a teenager in the late 1960s, having been born in 1953, it was hard not to be affected by and take an interest in what was going on in the community around me, and my family likewise would have taken an interest. And I suppose then when I went to Queen's in 1971 it was quite a frenetic time, particularly in the run-up to Bloody Sunday, the dissolution of Stormont, all of that. So it was pretty heavy politics, and that's where I would have had my baptism and initial involvement in politics: Queen's University.

Maybe in my subconscious as a child, politics had a place. My parents had actually been born in the Irish Republic. They had lived in County Monaghan and had only moved in 1949 or '50. I was always conscious of why they moved and what they perceived to be the Catholic Church's stranglehold on southern society and all of that, which probably made me quite aware of what the whole talk about a united Ireland was all about. They certainly didn't ram it down my throat, but it was there, and any questions you wanted to ask were answered.

Certainly both my parents were quite robust and strong in their unionist outlook; I'm sure some of that rubbed off on me and I have no regrets about that. I think I'm still fundamentally a very convinced unionist. I think political events, and the manifestation of devolution that we have now, which is shambolic and dysfunctional, would have reduced my enthusiasm about devolution. So to that extent, my political views, I suppose, have changed. But the fundamentals are as they were. I'm sure if I sat and thought about it I could come up with nuances of change in my thinking, but nothing springs to mind.

In terms of my interest in politics, I was studying law, and for many people there's a nexus between law-making and the practice of law; that those who are interested in politics tend to be interested in the law and vice versa. I was studying law and constitutional law at that particular time – one was, I'll not say a natural companion, but one was a complement to the other.

The Centenaries

As to the signing of the Covenant, I don't think the ideals have been maintained as sufficiently as they ought to have been. The core belief that underscored the Ulster Covenant was equal citizenship, and yet we've arrived a hundred years on in a scenario where some of the most basic tenets of equal citizenship in a democracy are denied to us. The right to change your government – we're not allowed that in Northern Ireland because of the absurdities of mandatory coalition. The right to have an opposition. Things that are taken for granted, which might seem pretty basic to any concept of equal citizenship, which might seem basic to any concept of democracy, have been trimmed back, if not obliterated. So I think the core principle hasn't flourished the way I would like to have seen. In fact it has been suppressed – and some of that self-inflicted. Unionists, by buying into that concept of the Belfast Agreement, which suppresses the right to have an opposition, the democratic right to change your government, have brought that upon themselves.

If we look at the signing of the Ulster Covenant, I certainly think that the attachment to the union for me is still strong. I wonder sometimes, when I look around at what some unionists have been prepared to settle for, whether it matters to them as much as I would like it to matter.

They have settled for incredible propositions; we're supposed to be an integral part of the United Kingdom but we're not allowed to change our government, we're not allowed to have an opposition. In fact, we must have in government those whose organisations set about murdering and butchering us. As of right! Those seem to me light years away from the principles that underscored the Ulster Covenant. I think if you were to say to anyone who signed the Ulster Covenant in 1912 that, a hundred years hence, manifestation of those whose politics you fear will be effectively ruling over you, as of right, and you will not be allowed to have an opposition against them, and you'll not be allowed to put them out of government or change your government – they would say, 'That's not what we're signing the Ulster Covenant for, it's the very antithesis of what we're signing the Ulster Covenant for.' So I think the whole essence of British citizenship has been so suppressed and distorted by the Belfast Agreement that though we remain a part of the United Kingdom, in a notional way and in a more than notional way constitutionally, we do not enjoy the rights of citizenship that everyone else takes for granted.

I would like a commemoration of the signing of the Covenant to produce a rebirth within unionism, a belief in the fundamentals of equal citizenship and a facing-up to the fact that we've had a lot taken away from us. But I suspect that many will be to the fore, paying lip-service to the commemoration of the events, and won't want their own consciences pricked by drawing attention to just how far they have departed. That's why I suspect there will be every effort made to keep the focus off the absence of citizenship – the absence of British citizenship which we once espoused.

If I had control of the 1912 commemoration, I think I would do it by way of compare and contrast. This is what the Covenant espoused to, this is what you got. Now, I don't think it would take much exposition to show just how far away we've drifted from the cardinal tenets of the Ulster Covenant.

I was always aware, coming from a family whose grandparents were signatories in County Monaghan of the Covenant, of the sense of betrayal that many had, that nine counties was reduced to six. I can perceive, from what I heard from my parents and grandparents, etc., that that was a tangible feeling for them. I can well understand that. My grandparents weren't alive when I was interested in exploring those issues, sadly, but my father talked about how my grandparents had signed the Covenant and the sense of resigned resentment that the unionists of Monaghan were, in the end, let down in their terms.

I doubt if the commemoration will change public thinking about unionism. For some, the contrast between what they've settled for and what they've aspired to is so great, they will be wanting to get these commemorations over with. I think the big political parties who will have an influence and control will be wanting to get them over with, fundamentally. I think there are big issues there that should attract the public imagination. But, when you look back four months ago, people voted for all that they've got. Then it's hard to persuade yourself that they'll be suddenly inspired, much as I would like to think they would be, by rediscovering the essence of their unionism.

I think it's very important to commemorate the Battle of the Somme. I had a great-uncle who died at the Somme – my father's uncle. And I think most families – and not just from the unionist community – have someone in their genealogy who paid the sacrifice. The Somme was such a horrendous event in terms of the scale of the sacrifice, that it's burnt into the psyches of many people in Northern Ireland. It is a fascinating story, in that those who were preparing themselves to resist Home Rule and to take on the British authorities ended up doing as was their natural inclination – serving the empire. And suffering so grievously in a single battle and with losses so huge. If you translated that forward to today, it must have been a huge loss. If you were to switch on your television and hear that X thousands of people had died in a battle … I think sometimes we hear so much about war, and so much of it seems so distant. Yes, we see people coming home and bodies and families grieving, but the scale – I mean, war is not a pretty thing. The scale of the loss right across Northern Ireland was huge, so I think it is burnt into the psyche very much.

Despite that, I think it is necessary to commemorate it. Just as we do on Remembrance Day, likewise on the first of July, I believe it is important to celebrate the lives of those who sacrificed so much, and to give them their due place in our history and in shaping our history. I think that certainly is important.

Is there any sense of irony among unionism that the very forces they were preparing to resist to avoid Home Rule, they fought alongside? No, I think that's a measure of their devotion to the union. Of course there's irony in every area of life if you analyse things in a certain way, but I think the fact that when the call came, they responded so magnanimously, was indicative that, in the hearts of them all, they were true unionists.

In the south, there has been some recognition of the fact that there were many people from there who, in the Great War, did equally sacrifice. For many years, shamefully, that was a closed book – it was as if those people didn't exist. I think it's right that in more recent times there has been recognition of that. So yes, there seems to be a willingness to acknowledge the history in that regard, and that has to be good.

I wouldn't want to see the Battle of the Somme or any other anniversary hijacked for the politics of the day. We've seen that so much, in the selling of the Belfast Agreement, from Bono and John Hume and all the rest in the Waterfront Hall, and every bandwagon being used to sell the latest political message. I don't want to see a solemn occasion like remembering the Battle of the Somme being turned into a political circus. If the people in the Republic feel enthused to celebrate and mark those who donned the British uniform, then that's a welcome thing. But my fear is, if you start massaging commemorations for political purposes, then they lose their real purpose. Joint celebration? There'll be celebrations open to everyone. Just as the joining of the British Army was open to everyone, and thankfully many of both persuasions did join it. So I don't think you have to go about and create some sort of artificial ambience for all of this. Either there is something there worth celebrating or there isn't.

And if there are official events commemorating the signing of the Covenant and the Battle of the Somme, I anticipate attending those. If I were invited to a commemoration of the Battle of the Somme in the south? I'd have to be totally convinced that it was an apolitical motivation. They'd have their work cut out to do so! [*Laughs*] So let's wait and see. At the moment, I don't anticipate circumstances where there would be that apolitical type of event that would persuade me that I wasn't being used.

In terms of the effect of commemoration, I think first and foremost people should have an intensified awareness of the sacrifice that people made, and at the same time that war is not a glamorous thing, that war is a very serious business in which people lose their lives, but the cause in which they lost their lives was a just cause and a necessary cause, and therefore it's not something to be entered into lightly. But when it happens, when fate decreed that for that generation that was a price to be paid, those who willingly paid it deserve to be saluted for their courage, and for what they helped deliver to the rest of us. So I think it needs to be a sober reflection on what it all means and what it was for, and if there's a political spin-off, then for unionists I would like to think that it would bring home to them the affinity and the ties that our forefathers felt with the British, and that we might be inspired to emulate and not diminish that. I would like to see it strengthen the unionist outlook on life, but that's very much secondary to the proper, due respect for the price that those people paid.

In terms of linking it to the signing of the Covenant, I think there would be cross-fertilisation there. Because remember, a lot of people from the Protestant community who died at the Somme would have been signatories of the Ulster Covenant, and what they were affirming in the Covenant – their belief in the British link – was what they were then dying for, four years later.

I don't think we should be patronising anyone, and sometimes that's a line that's hard to draw. We should be saying to nationalists and republicans that just as many of their forebears, through the Irish divisions, were sacrificed at the Somme and later in the war, and that's something that they too can rightly take pride in. For too long that was expunged from the nationalist psyche, and that was a great disservice to those who had made that sacrifice. I think there is a message that there's no shame in the man who died wearing the uniform of the British Army, and to me, as a unionist, that the union has benefits for all, Catholic or Protestant. Their forefathers who made the voluntary sacrifice saw that, so maybe there's room for them to see that too. But it shouldn't be rammed down their throats in a patronising way.

As for Easter 1916, I have no doubt that already, from the Sinn Féin direction, just as they turn the Hunger Strike commemorations into big political events for their own political advantage, that there will be every attempt on their part to celebrate those they would see, in their terms, as their forefathers in the rebellion they have engaged in. To an extent they are entitled to do that as they wish. But likewise don't let them patronise me or ram it down my throat – or rewrite history or recreate them as some sort of heroes. In my book, they were rebels taking the opportunity, as the IRA often did, of Britain's extremity, to pursue a course of rebellion. And I don't want it sanitised and changed beyond the truth of what it was. They're not going to persuade me that those who took over the GPO did the right thing and that they were anything other than how I've described them. If they killed in the pursuit of their aim then yes, of course they were murderers, because they weren't regular troops, acting under the protection of a state of war. They were those engaged in an act of rebellion against the state which at that time ruled over them.

I think there will be a huge attempt to glamorise Easter 1916, that it will be the Sinn Féin aim to deepen a sense of republicanism throughout Ireland. But Ireland today is a much more secular, open place than it was a hundred years ago. So there will be more scepticism from some of the ordinary citizens of the Republic about the glamorising of it, etc. Although it is very much part of the constitutional psyche of the Irish Republic – because of the manner in which the 1916 events are officially celebrated and have been for many years – that these were some sort of patriot heroes cut down by the venomous hateful British. And if I were invited to participate in the Easter 1916 commemorations, I think you could assume 100 per cent that I would not be there.

As to inviting republicans or nationalists to commemorations of the signing of the Ulster Covenant for some tuning in to each other, I don't think it's a matter of tuning in. I think what is really being suggested is that we should so sanitise the Covenant signing, the Somme sacrifice, that we bleed it dry of any real significance and just make it some sort of anodyne thing that's way back in history and means nothing to anyone. That's not what it is at all. I think that would be the purpose of those who would dream that up. And of course for some in this building – we're sitting in Stormont – who day and daily prop up IRA/Sinn Féin in government, they might like to see, as a sort of conscience salver for themselves, a wider community spread of this embracing and equalising of the IRA and its history with British culture and history. Certainly I see a vast difference between the gallant men of the Somme and the opportunistic rebels of the General Post Office.

It could be argued that centenary commemorations will deepen division, but I think a nation who forgets its history loses its soul. I mean, what is it that makes any nation what they are? What is it that makes Americans what they are? It's the War of Independence and the Civil War, amongst other things. Now, no one would suggest to an American – and you notice we've just had the 9/11 commemorations – that in the interests of the overall collegiate good we should forget about all that, we shouldn't celebrate any of that or mark any of that. Likewise no one should suggest to me as a unionist that iconic historic events should not be marked in the way that they deserve, in deference to some nebulous thing which is called progress.

National identity has undoubtedly been blurred, and the whole ethos and *raison d'être* of the EU is, in time, to discard and obliterate national identities. But that process, which some have forecast, is beginning to fray and maybe unravel. It's a question of balance. Yes, of course we live in a smaller world today in the sense that there are interdependencies that are an essential part of life. But I certainly very strongly believe in the nation state, and in the rights of the nation state and in sustaining the nation state. And be the state the Irish state or the British state, I think due regard and respect for the celebration of our history is a part of that. That's why, if the people of Dublin and elsewhere want to celebrate the 1916 Rising, that's their business, they can do that. But equally if they can do that, so we in the United Kingdom can celebrate cardinal events such as the signing of the Covenant and the Battle of the Somme, which were themselves global – the Somme in particular.

I think it's a national thing. Yes you can break it down into unionism but I'm simply saying that I'm not being prescriptive to the Irish Republic and saying, 'Don't you celebrate something I wouldn't celebrate.' If they want to celebrate the 1916 Rising, they celebrate it, but please don't ram it down my throat.

BRIAN LEESON

Brian Leeson is chairman of éirigí, a socialist republican party formed in Dublin by a group of former Sinn Féin activists in 2006. Now thirty-seven years of age, Leeson has been active in republican politics since 1989, when he started selling the newspaper An Phoblacht *outside the GPO on Dublin's O'Connell Street. Before leaving Sinn Féin in 2006, Leeson held the position of National Organiser of that party.*

Background

The period I grew up in was the 1970s to the mid-'80s, so through the recession of the '80s I was coming into young adulthood and becoming conscious of the economic situation, combined with the conflict in the six counties, which was in full flow in that period. So yes, I think it would have been something of a political upbringing – certainly of a left perspective. We were a family where the Six O'Clock News would have been on, the evening radio show on RTÉ One would have been on; so it was a house where current affairs were discussed. Compared to some of my peers or neighbours or friends, I think I lived in a political household.

My father was in the Labour Party in the 1960s – but it would have been political with a small 'p'. Politics and current affairs were regularly discussed within the family; it was a house where kids were encouraged to ask questions and to stand up for what they believed in. My attendance for most of my primary schooling at a gaelscoil would have played some role in heightening my sense of Irishness. My first memory of being exposed to the conflict in the six counties was a family holiday in Donegal, which coincided with the 1981 Hunger Strike: black flags, bonfires on the beach with the Union Jack on top of them, marching in support of prisoners.

By the time I was into my teenage years I was awakening. The Hunger Strike epitomised for me what political struggle is about. I was filled with admiration for the sacrifice of those ten who died, all of those who joined the Hunger Strike and those who were on the blanket. I think it was a classic struggle between those who had nothing but their own bodies as weapons against a great imperial power. History hopefully will judge those men and that period kindly. I really think it was a very significant event in Irish history.

I think, probably like many republicans, I have now moved from a more one-dimensional nationalist outlook. There was a war taking place in this country. The focus of that was clearly on the British state. As I got older and as the situation de-escalated, I began to develop an interest in where the conflict in Ireland came from and see its roots in terms of a class struggle, an imperial struggle.

Brian Leeson

The Centenaries

The signing of the Ulster Covenant will be commemorated. As to whether it should or not, I'm not so sure. You have the Covenant, the formation of the Ulster Volunteers, the formation of the Irish Volunteers, the 1913 Lock-out, Easter 1916, the Tan War, the Civil War – it's a whole decade of centenaries, and many of them are inter-related.

To me, the Covenant was almost the defining point in an arms race between the unionist cause and the nationalist cause. The signing of the Covenant and the creation of the Ulster Volunteers, which are very much interlinked, and the creation of the Irish volunteers – that all developed over a couple of years, with both organisations moving quite rapidly into mass organisation, both equipping themselves with the weapons of war. I think the Covenant needs to be seen in the context of that. I come from the republican tradition. I don't think Ireland was well served by the Covenant, but I also think it's wider than that – leading into the issue of the Battle of the Somme and the First World War, and all of those centenaries coming up. Were working-class Protestants well served? That would be a question worth asking.

To me the Covenant was an example of how the unionist ruling class managed to co-opt the working class in behind them, to act in ways that are not necessarily in the interests of the working class – that the flag has been able to outplay the issue of class. What if the choice for working-class Protestants had been to be part of a new republic, which might have put the working class in the driving seat, versus remaining as the lower classes within a six-county state? The Covenant was another example of the unionist ruling class co-opting the working class into supporting political positions which may not actually have been in their class's interest – in effect, the playing of the Orange card and the whipping up of a sectarian frenzy. The Covenant was almost a club: if you had not joined you were somehow suspect. The idea of people allegedly signing it in their own blood – this was part of the whipping up of sectarian divisions and trying to isolate those who had not signed the Covenant. I would suspect that in some communities, if you had not signed it, you were subject to considerable suspicion and resentment; so I would wonder how many of those that signed it, signed it absolutely willingly. We'll probably never know. But the figure of a quarter of a million males who signed and a quarter of a million females who signed the female equivalent – that was a huge percentage of the population. It was a very visible parading of loyalty again, I believe, to whip people into sectarian lines which I don't think have been to the benefit of the working class.

Did what stemmed from the Covenant and that period – the partition of Ireland and, in effect, the creation of a largely Protestant-dominated state in the north and a largely Catholic-dominated state in the south – ultimately work to the benefit of those Protestant workers who signed the Covenant? That would be an interesting question and an interesting way of marking the anniversary, but certainly I don't think there's anything positive about it to be commemorated as a great event. To me it wasn't. It was highly regressive initiative, combined with the creation of the Ulster Volunteer Force in the same period, and in effect it was the threat of an armed insurrection by a minority of the population of this island to thwart the wishes of the majority of this island, leading to partition. So to me it was a largely negative event, and in commemorating it, we should be questioning who really benefited from the creation of the Covenant and all that flowed from it.

I would imagine unionists will commemorate it as a positive event of historical importance; something to be remembered with pride and enthusiasm. I would think the more hard-line elements of unionism would remember it in that way and see it as one of those critically important initiatives of that period, and therefore I imagine they would celebrate as well as commemorate. But obviously from a republican perspective, it's not something that'd be seen in a very positive light.

It's possible it'll lead to a deeper entrenchment of unionism. One of the factors to look at is what's happening in Scotland, and the potential for the unionist tradition in Ireland to interpret what's happening in Scotland as having the potential for the break-up of the so-called United Kingdom. The traditional response of unionism to any threat to the union has been violence against the Catholic community and the ratcheting up of sectarianism. It could happen. Potentially this anniversary could be used as an example of how unionism previously faced down a British Government and faced down the democratic will of the people of this island. We remember the 1966 commemoration of the 1916 events, and indeed the centenary of the '98 Rising; these anniversaries have an impact on the contemporary situation. So I think it's conceivable it could result in increased entrenchment. But I think that would be more determined by the perceived present threat to the union. What is happening in Scotland may catapult that reactionary element back into unionism, and in that context it could be very dangerous. Does it become something that's marked on every street corner or is it going to be the preserve of a couple of historical societies? That's all to be determined over the course of the year, whether it becomes an on-the-street event, in which case it could be potentially dangerous, and particularly dangerous for isolated Catholic communities.

There will be two general trends in the commemoration of Easter 1916. One will be the state commemorative events, which will be very politics-free, in that they will market Easter 1916 as an important historical event that led to the creation of the twenty-six-county state. But there will be no or very little recognition by the state and by the establishment of the six counties issue – of the British Government's presence and claim to jurisdiction over the six counties. This will not feature on the official commemorative programme. It'll be very much focused on a sort of solemn commemorative event, which will no doubt take place over a couple of days and will as quickly as possible be forgotten about.

The second aspect will be the people themselves, non-state-commemorative events, and that's where it's going to be potentially a lot more interesting. That's where more questions will be asked, comparisons made between the 1916 vision and the reality of today. As you know, the 1916 Proclamation was riddled, not just with the politics of national liberation, but also with the politics of equality and challenging of the status quo. I think you'll find that the non-governmental events will focus more on that comparison, and from my own perspective and from éirígí's perspective, we will highlight how little has been achieved since 1916 and how much of the programme of 1916 remains to be achieved.

I think it will be that two-tier commemoration. The official state programme will be very much focused on the creation of this state, as opposed to the liberation of the country. These are two very different things, the state and the country, and the majority of the focus of the state and the establishment will be on an interesting and important historical event, but very much historical – comparison should not be made with today. The non-governmental will focus more on, yes, commemorating and celebrating 1916 Rising, but also on the unfinished business, both in terms of the national question and the socio-economic one. I mean, no one could suggest that James Connolly or many of the other Citizen Army volunteers – or indeed, in fairness, the IRB volunteers – did not have a radical social and economic programme as well as one for national liberation. They certainly had both.

None of us can be slaves to history, and each generation, and within each generation, there must be the ability to critically analyse the contemporary world. You can't just take a template from ten years ago or fifty years ago, or indeed a hundred years ago, and try and impose it on contemporary Ireland. But that said, I think that within the Proclamation and within the democratic programme of the first Dáil, which will be having its centenary in 2019, are the core values of freedom, of equality, of justice, of fairness – these are timeless. I don't think the idea of equality gets old; it may go out of fashion but I don't think it loses its intrinsic value or importance. Some of the language of the 1916 Proclamation may not be appropriate today, but the writings and political agitation organisations that had gone on the previous ten years as well – the Labour movement, the 1913 Lock-out, the suppression of workers by the state just three years before the 1916 Rising, the whole melting pot that was the 1916 Rising and the various trends that came together in the GPO that morning – to me many of the values they espoused and many of the demands they had are timeless. The demand for freedom and the demand for equality – they are timeless, and I think there's a huge amount within the 1916 document, and within the programme of those radicals and revolutionaries, that remains to be achieved and is still valid today.

The state in an ideal world would be marking the occasion as a national celebration; not a commemoration, a celebration. In any other nation in this world – France with Bastille Day, the US with the Fourth of July – I mean name your country, it's a national holiday, it's an event with major parades and so forth. But I also think that huge work could be done in terms of schools, in terms of younger people; a national debate, a genuine discussion at a very local level, at a very participative level, as to how today compares to the Ireland that was envisaged in Easter 1916, the Ireland that they sought to create. And hopefully coming out of that would be a more educated, more politicised population which might be more inclined to demand those basic rights that were called for by the likes of Connolly and Pearse – beyond the national question to the social question, the rights of women, of minorities, the distribution of wealth and power. When you read some of the writings of 100 years ago, they seem so radical by today's standards and the contemporary society in which we live. The demands of trade unions, the first Dáil calling for land reform, the reorganisation of industry – these were very radical demands almost a century ago, and that would be a really interesting discussion. In the current climate, where the IMF and EU are in control of the twenty-six counties and the British state is still in control of the six counties, I think that would be a really interesting conversation to have. And I mean a genuine discussion, not just a half-hour chat show on RTÉ One; a really participative process across the country. That would be one way to mark the 1916 Rising.

The core analysis that radical republicans would hold, that I would hold, is that the 1916 Rising was not just about national freedom; it was also about a social and economic revolution within the power relations of the state, as well as the issue of the British occupation. And that, in essence, the counter-revolutionary forces which formed around the Treaty elements – the majority of the Catholic Church, the majority of the business class, and those who had never supported the idea of Irish freedom, who rallied in behind the pro-Treaty faction – won out in the Civil War and what developed in the twenty-six counties was a counter-revolutionary state that very quickly moved to quite a traditional model, in terms of how power and politics were distributed. It was pretty much a Catholic state for a Catholic people along traditional capitalist European lines. That's how the state evolved and developed. So for me, as a republican, I think the Easter Rising 1916 anniversary could be used to reignite the thought of a people's revolution and to re-examine what actually happened in that period – that hugely important period from 1916-1922, where the potential for an Irish revolution emerged and was ultimately suppressed – and the outcomes, ninety years later. I think we need the discussion of that idea, to ask whether the demands of that revolution are valid today. With sovereignty being handed over to the International Monetary Fund and to the European Union, I think a lot more people now – more than five years ago even – would be open to the idea that the demands of that revolution, that potential revolution, were not so radical after all; that they were quite reasonable demands and that those demands remain valid to this day. I think that would be a really suitable and fitting way to commemorate those who fought and died in '16.

The Proclamation covered the island of Ireland, and the 1918 election was on an all-Ireland basis, so it's about an analysis of Ireland as a whole; how both states have emerged. I don't think anybody could claim that the Ireland we have today is the Ireland that was envisaged in the 1916 Proclamation. But given that the Rising was a Dublin-based event and it would be the Dublin government that would be holding the official state commemorations, I think that the questions would probably be best put to that state as opposed to the part of the country that remains under British jurisdiction. To some extent, those who remain under British jurisdiction have not had a chance to create an Ireland of their own making, whereas it's arguable that the twenty-six counties had the opportunity to break with the past and create a radically different and a radically better society and they chose not to.

Will the commemoration of the Rising make a lasting difference? It's definitely too early to tell, given that the event hasn't occurred [*Laughs*], but I think there is historic precedent. Historians point to the hundredth anniversary of the 1798 Rising in 1898 as a critical igniter of nationalist sentiment. The celebrations that took place in 1898, some would say, actually bore fruit eighteen years later with the 1916 Rising.

Similarly, many would say the events in 1966 for the fiftieth anniversary of 1916 brought the politics of national freedom back to centre stage again and potentially had an impact in raising national sentiment within the twenty-six counties. History shows that when such dramatic events occurred in '68, '69, '70, the initial response of the south was to support the nationalist community in the north and those who were demanding a British withdrawal. As we know, that was quickly reversed by the mid-'70s, but certainly, again, historians have pointed to the fact that the fiftieth anniversary of 1916 had a radicalising effect on that generation. So no matter how much the state try to control it, no matter how much the state try to downplay the importance of the hundredth anniversary, it is quite possible that the hundredth anniversary will radicalise a new generation and bring a new generation into contact with the politics of 1916, and with the radical politics of Connolly and Pearse, and those ideas may again find fertile ground 100 years later. Again, in the current context of the EU/IMF and the depression that is visiting this state at this point, it may prove to be one of a series of radicalising events of this period.

At this point, what is achievable and necessary is the creation and strengthening of the radical trend in the Irish political system. That radical trend at this point is clearly very weak. Given the context of the economic situation, the radical forces in this state and also in the six counties have been ill-equipped to offer solutions to the average person. I think that is where the focus is for radicals: the radicalisation, the spreading of that political message and attempting to garner mass support behind the radical demands that '16 represented. Could it potentially lead to people taking armed actions? Of course it could. I mean there are people taking armed actions today. But will it lead to a mass armed insurrection? I've no way of knowing. What we would be looking for would be a much bigger number of people becoming politicised and exposed to the ideas behind the 1916 Rising, and supporting those ideas.

As for the Somme, there's no doubt that for many of those from a nominally nationalist tradition who fought and died – not just at the Somme but in the entire First World War – the twenty-six counties was a cold house and a cold state, and the same goes for the relatives of those who were killed. I think there has been somewhat of a shift in the way that the state and the establishment, and people generally, view those who joined the British Army at that point. I think it's well documented that there has been a softening of attitude towards that.

I think the Somme will more than likely be commemorated with a series of Masses and religious or non-religious commemorative events, which I imagine will receive plenty of publicity and support from the establishment. I don't see it as having the potential for a mass commemorative event, where tens of thousands of people are going to come out to stand at the side of the road to take part, to participate in a ceremony in commemoration of those who died, whereas I think the potential for that exists with regard to the 1916 Rising.

The fact is that tens of thousands of young Irish men – almost exclusively men, I believe – died in the First World War, and they went to fight in that war – and primarily joined the British army – for a wide variety of reasons. There were those who went there at the behest of Irish nationalist leaders who told them they were fighting for the rights of small nations, and many of them believed that they were. And there were those who went at the behest of the leaders of unionism, who told them that they were fighting for Ulster, and if they didn't go and fight they would face extermination within some Catholic Home Rule state that would very quickly discriminate against them. Both of those blocs of people were misled. Working-class Protestants, primarily from the six counties, and working-class Catholics, primarily from the twenty-six counties, as they are now within the lines of partition, were both led a merry dance by their respective leaders and went to die in a war which was about the ego of men and imperial empires, and the ambitions of Britain and Germany and Austro-Hungary and Russia and all those old powers of Europe. It was a tragedy. Anyone who has walked the graveyards or battlefields of Europe couldn't forget. You'd want a heart of stone not to be affected by the mass slaughter of working-class German and working-class British lads, who would have been far better served using those guns to challenge the ruling powers in their own nations, and far better served by standing up and organising change within their own countries, as opposed to being led down the war-path of jingoism and the romantic notion of a war for small nations, which history has shown as nothing but lies, nonsense.

I think it unlikely that we will commemorate the Somme. It's not something that we as an organisation have discussed, but I would know from informal chat to republicans that many people would see that whole period as a tragedy and that the deaths were pointless, worthless – so that's how it would be marked. Certainly one could mark the sadness, mark the tragedy of that, and so on. But from our perspective as republicans, given that there is not capacity to mark every event, the focus will be on the likes of the 1916 Rising. The Somme is one particular battle, but Irishmen died in lots of battles in the First World War. All of those people who are lying in graves in France and Belgium – all of their centenaries are coming up. Insomuch as we choose to mark that, it would be – and I'm only speculating – in terms of debate or discussion or a public talk about what the First World War was all about and why all these unionists and nationalists, Catholics and Protestants marched off to meet the German guns. What did it achieve and why did they go?

It would certainly not be a celebration or endorsement of what those imperial powers were about at that point. It can be difficult to separate it out and the danger – or maybe the challenge – would be for people to separate the plight of working-class Protestants from Belfast or working-class Catholics from Dublin, who found themselves in British uniforms fighting German uniforms, from the jingoism and the triumphalism of the great powers of that time. Certainly that would be my own perspective: that the whole period was a tragedy for Ireland.

I would hope that the outworking of these centenaries would be the introduction of a new generation – or the reintroduction for those of us who are older – to the core ideas of what the progressive elements of that time were about, and that more people would come on board with the progressive ideas of that time. Because there were many progressive ideas and there were many regressive ideas, and no one community has an absolute monopoly on either. But the more progressive elements – whether the few should rule the many or the many should rule the many – were at the core of what the republican struggle was about in 1916, and what the republican struggle is about today. I would be optimistic that the outworking of this period will be positive; that it will see a new generation introduced to and embracing some of those ideas, many of which are not just a hundred years old, they're many hundreds of years old.

TIM PAT COOGAN

Tim Pat Coogan is a historical writer, broadcaster and newspaper columnist. He was editor of the Irish Press *from 1968 to 1987. His books on modern Irish history include* The IRA, On the Blanket, *and biographies of Michael Collins and Éamon de Valera.*

Background

I was reared in the upper-middle-class suburb of Monkstown, south County Dublin, and I've lived in that area all my life. My father was a Fine Gael TD and general secretary of the party. He died when I was very young, but I remember election campaigns and talk of politics. My mother's father was born in the South Armagh area, and he couldn't get any advancement in the north because he was a Catholic. So he came down here and joined the RIC. And he ran a post office. He got burned out by the IRA so he was then out of sync in two jurisdictions. He wound up taking his revenge on Catholic, Protestant and Dissenter by becoming the Chief Income Tax Collector for the counties of Dublin and Wicklow.

My earliest political memories would be in my father's parents' house in Castlecomer, County Kilkenny. They had a pub and a bit of land, which my grandfather Tim Coogan made a smaller bit of land by assiduously attending to his thirst. My father had an excellent library and a very strong nationalist library. As quite a small boy I learned about figures in Irish history that you wouldn't learn about in school, like Cahir O'Doherty or Galloping O'Hogan, and obviously the great O'Neill, Sarsfield, and figures like Parnell. So I had a strong grasp on Irish history, from a nationalist perspective, I suppose, but I broadened that out. I was always interested in history and in writing; and living here on the east coast, you got BBC broadcasts and television when nobody else did, and that was a kind of window on the world, seeing ministers being put on the spot in current affairs programmes, and so on.

So I'd a variegated background, and I went into the *Evening Press* when it was founded. Vivian de Valera remembered me speaking at a debate in Blackrock College and a mentor of mine at Blackrock, Fr Carroll, a history teacher, rang him up and said that he had a boy who would either turn out a genius or break his heart. I regretfully never managed either. But anyway I graduated – or fell, whichever way you like to put it – from the *Evening Press* to become editor of the *Irish Press,* which had been founded by de Valera, and I stayed in the firm. One way and another I was nearly thirty-five years there.

The Centenaries

I'm glad the three centenaries are taking place. I know our government are, behind the scenes, in contact with the unionists about a proper celebration of all three. There really is a recognition that you have to look at Irish history in the round. Home Rule, remember, was acquiesced to by the Irish electorate as a whole, by a majority of some 5-1 in cases, from 1886 onwards. But it didn't get anywhere until the eve of the First World War. And by then armed resistance to the parliamentary process had been re-established by the Ulster Volunteers. Carson told them not to worry about illegalities – 'I'll look after you' – and the Conservative leader Bonar Law told the unionists at the famous Balmoral meeting that he could imagine no lengths to which the Ulsterman would go that the Conservatives would not support them.

The Covenant and the Larne gun-running made 1916 inevitable, so I think it's a seamless garment. Now I don't know whether I would use the word 'celebrate' for any of the three centenaries; I would use the word 'commemorate'. I am an unashamed Irish nationalist and I believe in a united Ireland, so I would prefer that the Ulster Volunteers had not been formed and that there had been no gun-running. It hadn't been made very clear to the nationalist population of Ireland that the army *and* the navy, apart from the Conservatives, weren't going to implement Home Rule on what we now know as the six counties.

As to commemoration, I think things should be done with dignity and with understanding that it's part of a historical process. That should be the *leitmotif* of the unionist component of this dialogue, just as much as the nationalists. I certainly don't think that any nationalist should try to make the signing of the Covenant an occasion for assault on the unionist tradition or the unionist community, or to in any way disrupt the Good Friday Agreement process.

People take a very simplistic, 'today's-headline or soundbite' view of history. When Martin McGuinness decided to go into southern politics at the time of the presidential election, the seagulls rose up in the media and there was tremendous denunciation, as if this were something extraordinarily foreign to Irish politics. Every single party on the island entered the democratic arena or the parliament with a gun in its pocket or else at home in the store. And that included the unionists, the Labour party, and of course the various strands of Irish party. Both Fine Gael and de Valera and his people, came into the Dáil with guns. I think that the unionists have to recognise that.

As we know, as a result of the gun-running – Covenant first, gun-running second – Home Rule was shelved. And against a background of the Famine and the defiance by the Ulstermen, the nationalist Volunteers struck and you had 1916. After that, as the pot was boiling again post-war, this very important Irish sub-committee of the Cabinet met. You can see the papers, they're still there in the Public Record Office in London, and it's quite obvious they were all very surprised. Lloyd George returned from a meeting with Sir James Craig, where he told Lloyd George that, surprisingly, he doesn't want Ulster, he wants six counties of Ulster, because they can't control nine counties, they can only control six.

The Ulster Covenant defiance meant that there was going to be partition, that there was going to be a six-county northern state, but the British assumed it would be a nine-county state. The word 'Ulster' denotes nine, and they assumed that nobody would be more keen on this than the unionists. But Sir James said no, they could only control six. And where that threw a shadow, which still exists today, was this word 'control'. They were afraid that the citadel would fall to the Papishes within – to the Catholics with a superior birth-rate and their allegiance to the Republic in the south (although it wasn't a republic then). So they made it a state where they would be safe by using the laws to discriminate and gerrymander constituencies against the Catholics. It was intended that they would have an upper chamber, which would give the Papishes some sort of say in the north, and they would have PR, but they knocked both those things out because they had this siege mentality, a citadel mentality.

Today, when you come to commemorate these things, remember something else has happened. Their control has been confirmed peaceably by the Good Friday Agreement. And although they are dealing, initially very reluctantly, with the Dublin Government, they no longer feel that this is no business of theirs: the Dublin Government is at the table as of right. They've seen that Britain has allowed some of the sovereignty or some of the entitlement of Dublin to flow into Belfast. You had the Secretariat and you still have the joint North–South bodies. They're not very important but they're a sign, and it's quite clear from the rapprochement of the political system – not of every member, but of people like Paisley and Martin McGuinness – that times have moved. They're huge changes.

It's like the Irish rosary beads of old, where you had the decades of the rosary and in the middle, after every ten, you had the 'Our Father', the bigger bead. These were sort of stepping stones along the rosary. Well three of the important stepping stones along the way – which tragically led to a lot of bloodshed but are there or were there and have to be recognised – were these three commemorations.

One would hope unionists will look afresh at 1912 and won't make it an occasion of triumphalism. Nobody can say with certainty. But I would have thought that, looking at the temper of modern unionism and the more emollient sounds coming from unionism, they would commemorate their history with some dignity but not necessarily with triumphalism. I mean, the more intelligent of them must have seen where triumphalism got them with the Orange marches. Drumcree has faded into the past, but look at what it meant, because it's most symbolic. They wanted to march where they had always marched, which was open fields. Those open fields are Catholic housing estates today – culturally, I mean. And they know the greatest criticism voiced on this island of the Catholic Church comes from Catholics, over paedophilia and other scandals. So what I would dearly like to see would be these commemorations, both by Orange and Green, being viewed as part of a tapestry, not as the citadel defended or the island fortress held. And that on the tapestry they would have to concede the flow of history; how they came to have a Protestant garrison – a Praetorian guard, whatever you may call it – and why the Conservatives would make an alliance with them, because in fact they made it with them for purely political party advantage.

Anyone would have thought it incredible, some years ago, to think of the Queen being at the Garden of Remembrance, or to watch an Irish President running over to kiss Iris Robinson, with her husband, the hero of Clontibret, attending presumably on behalf of all the people of the six counties. Yet that happened in Dublin. The signing of the Covenant centenary would primarily be an Orange celebration – a Protestant and unionist one – but I presume that they would make space … I mean, the admission by Trimble that the six counties had been a cold house for nationalists – which you'd think is a self-evident admission, but nevertheless he made it – seems to indicate that the next logical step over the coming years would be to make the house warm, to have some sort of a welcome sign somewhere in the house – a fáilte. I imagine it would only be neighbourly and dignified modern political behaviour for the unionist organisers of this to invite southern visitors, certainly to invite the MLAs of the Sinn Féin party to it, and that all parties would comport themselves with dignity.

But 1916 will be the biggest one, I'd imagine. I would think that the nationalist element will have to exercise great restraint. Now, obviously both north and south there'll be parades and special trains laid on and so on; I hope that when people get off that train, they'll get off it sober in Belfast and that they won't be met by stone-throwers. One of Paisley's achievements in the early days which gave him great publicity was to get the trains from the south halted as they came north. I hope nothing like that will happen and I hope that groups such as, for want of a better term, the Real IRA, or what we call dissidents nowadays – the remnants of the physical force tradition in republicanism – will behave themselves and not take action, or certainly not military action.

I most definitely think unionists should be invited to the Easter 1916 commemorations. I very often find it difficult to invade the mind of a nationalist politician, or those of the Fine Gael or Fianna Fáil stripe, so to take over the interior working of Mr Poots' ... I suppose I can call it intellectual activity – I find that rather unfathomable. But the political situation is evolving so fast. Cast your mind back to the commemoration of the Treaty, the most seminal document in the twentieth century – probably in any century – in Ireland, which passed with barely a nod to it. Why? Because Europe was the focus. We're in Europe now. And the six counties may think they're extraneous to all the crises in the euro and southern Ireland; they're not. They can go down the tubes even further and faster than the south can.

We have lost a good deal of sovereignty in the Republic. It's shaming and it's a fact – and a highly dangerous thing. I'm currently working on a book on the Famine and I don't have to be told what not having a government of your own can lead to, when you have to apply to bureaucrats in another country for crumbs from the rich man's table. The situation calls for quite a different attitude.

You saw recently where there was an outburst of the old ways of doing things between the Shinners and the unionists: if you won't go to my football match, I won't go to yours, or I won't stand for your anthem, and so on. Then you have that laughable situation in the Irish rugby team where the unionist or Protestant element won't stand or they object to standing for the national anthem. Even though the English team would come over here and they'd be respectfully accorded a silence when they sing 'God Save The Queen' – even at Croke Park. Now if that kind of spirit manifests itself, it will not pass off well. But the rugby analogy is not a bad one to take because the reality of the situation is (and it's reality we're concerned with now) that those boys from the north – those stout Orange blades – they don't object to taking the Green cheque. And we're talking about cheques now, we're talking about money.

You've got to make this country as attractive as you can for business, for tourism, north and south. And for a long time, the south – through our official tourist boards – has been making packages which include the north. There should be more of that. The northern business boards, whatever they are, should see the advantage of combining with the Irish development board, the IDA, because there is obviously a pay-off. The way to do that would be to have tourists come along to see this pageantry, and there'd be, I dare say, the occasional libation to the gods afterwards, and there'd be a bit of music and craic. I'd like that kind of craic – not the crack of rifles and guns. I think it's elementary that that's the way they should all be celebrated.

As to the Somme, a change is taking place as we speak. There are some people who don't approve of the Irish Government and Army taking part in such commemorations, but a younger generation doesn't feel like that. They don't see any abrogation of unity in acknowledging that so many Irishmen fell in that battle. I think there is a valid intellectual argument that they were misled and that they fell in an imperial war while they thought that they were defending plucky little Belgium or that in some way it was going to help the Irish Home Rule movement. Birrell wrote an obituary of John Redmond, and he said something to the effect that when Redmond espoused the war and committed the Volunteers to it, his train took the curve too rapidly. They were quite clear about it – almost cynical – but it was all dressed up in patriotism and drums and so forth, just as the other side dressed up what they did in drums and so on. But it's not a time for anybody – and media commentators have a special role here – to be harping on about old grievances or taking one side or the other. I think you should recognise there were brave people on both sides and that according to their lights, they were doing the right thing.

I think the public attitude in the north and the south will have advanced after these commemorations. But I think the vibrancy of the nationalist tradition is not going to be halted. Just take the GAA. Unionists' public representatives might state for their more die-hard supporters that they wouldn't go to a GAA match, but you can't overlook the energy and the sheer weight of numbers at these matches. And the change in identity, in confidence. Take Ballymena, the Reverend's constituency, with places like Harryville, where they were picketing Mass. Indeed, an ex-Irish rugby international – wasn't he involved in those protests at Harryville? In my younger days going up to the north, there wouldn't be the slightest remote possibility of seeing young nationalists, Catholics, on the road with hurling sticks, or going to a football match with obvious GAA gear. They'd be rousted by the RUC; they'd be lucky to escape a kicking. And now what do you find? You find that the PSNI have joined in football matches with them. Popular culture and sport have a really important part to play.

I don't say that people shouldn't emphasise their own tradition. But they should do it by behaving with dignity. By all means go and commemorate, but don't come back at night half full and throw stones at your Catholic neighbours' windows. And I hope no fiery preachers on either side see a way to political advancement by extolling hatred or creating sectarian tension. But it's all to play for. Everything I say, I'm saying, 'I hope this' and 'I hope that'. The commemorations are only part of an on-going process. You've got to bear in mind the sensitivity of Irish history. I was a member of the government's National Famine Committee. We used to meet in the Taoiseach's buildings. For years I tried to get a Famine Commission meeting north of the border but there was resistance. Partly because of these commemorations and partly because there is still a residual feeling in Ulster Protestantism that the Famine was the result of Irish fecklessness; they brought it on themselves so why should they have a commemoration north of the border? Finally, as a result – possibly I'd something to do with it, possibly not – a commemoration was conceded in Ulster. And going back to Sir James Craig, where did they hold it? Clones, County Monaghan. But the Famine visited everybody. I mean, there's a huge cemetery in Cliftonville of Famine victims and they're all Protestant. They died of fever, which, by the way, was brought over by the Protestants from Scotland.

Unionist apologists would say that the commemoration of the fiftieth anniversary of the Rising led to the Troubles, and Paisley took advantage of them to help unhorse O'Neill. And the two boys Ward and Scullion were shot because of that, and this perfervid atmosphere. But that was how many years ago – fifty? We've had thirty years of death and destruction in between, and I hope we've all seen the folly of that. We've seen the way out via the Good Friday Agreement. Yes, there is sensitivity.

But time moves on. We're human beings, we're not dinosaurs. Granted these things happened, granted they're part of the warp and woof of Irish history, but if you look at them as a continuum, they all had a place in the history of Ireland. They should all be recognised. Recognising your identity, and being secure enough in it to commemorate, and your neighbour being secure enough to allow you to commemorate, is surely a sign of maturity and of strength, not of weakness.

Going back to the thing of Craig and Lloyd George, and the surprise of the British side when they found that he only wanted six of the counties – that was basically out of fear. They could only control six. You can call it neo-colonialism, but whatever you call it it was out of fear in the end. Now that fear has demonstrably lessened. The recognition by the south of the north, everything that's enshrined in the Good Friday Agreement, tells you that there shouldn't be problems.

There's no reason why people shouldn't commemorate their identity, their Irishness. If you're at a St Patrick's Day parade in any part of the world, you can see the strength of the nationalist tradition. I was on a platform in Trafalgar Square a couple of years back for a Paddy's Day commemoration, and the entire square was jam-packed, absolutely jam-packed. There was a continuous procession between the square behind our stage, which stretched right back, way up to the park where they were assembling, and as I was speaking, and as the procession was *en route* and the packed crowd stood in front of me there, there was some 50,000 people still waiting to get in to join it.

Unionists have got to recognise that it's not going to go away because you're alarmed. Are you going to adjust to it? Or what will you do with your alarm? Are you going to do what Gusty Spence did and take out a gun and shoot a barman? Or are you going to do what Gusty Spence did, slowly and painfully, over the years, and evolve into a situation of tolerance? I think you have to recognise in all this – I think you can take it as a given – that I can't see modern Sinn Féin being triumphalist over 1916. I certainly can't see the Dublin Government being allowed to by the electorate. But the manifestation of your own identity is not to deny somebody else their identity. And there is a Green tide. The fact is that there are hundreds and thousands of people between Croke Park and Casement Park, and six counties teams have been winning All-Irelands. I mean look at Tyrone, Derry, Armagh – all those places. There is a message in it. And the message is, as Parnell said many, many years ago: no man can set a barrier to the onward march of a nation.

NIALL O'DOWD

Niall O'Dowd is the founder and publisher of the Irish Voice and IrishCentral.com in the United States. He was extensively involved in the negotiations leading to the Good Friday Agreement.

Background

Politics was part of my upbringing. My father was an unreconstructed de Valera-ite who was hugely passionate about Fianna Fáil, and I grew up in a house where political discussion was very much part of the everyday experience. My mother was less so, but interestingly enough, one of my brothers is a TD, another was Mayor of Drogheda, one sister is active in Fine Gael, and the other is active in Fianna Fáil – so we were very politicised from a very early age.

I particularly remember the outbreak of the Troubles in the north. The day I saw my father angriest in his life was Bloody Sunday. He wasn't a man who got hugely angry about politics most of the time, but on that day he was absolutely incandescent with rage. You got the sense of a generation thing; he was born in 1906, and he had memories of the War of Independence and the Civil War, so it was very much a revisiting of all that emotion. My father was very pro- what was happening on the nationalist side: 'We Shall Overcome' and later on Sinn Féin and all of that.

My view of Irish politics has evolved over the years. When I was young I was very much of the opinion that de Valera was right about the Civil War and all that. Now as I get older and get more experience and less certain of myself, I can see Michael Collins's point of view: take what you can at this point and then build on the rest of it. It's a complicated history, Irish history, and it's something I keep learning about. Having the perspective from America is very helpful too, in that you're not immediately involved in the day-to-day and you can see it as a series of events; that if things had gone differently we would have had a very different country. Outcomes turned on things like a stray bullet that killed Collins in 1922, and it absolutely changed the whole future of the Irish at that moment. So it's fascinating history.

Actually, I think we in the States understand Ireland better than people here. Ours is a radical history. It started with the Famine. We funded the Fenian uprising, we funded the 1916 Rising. The great wave of emigration of the 1920s was of people who were fleeing the Irish Civil War and the War of Independence. Our view all along was that the fundamentals needed to be addressed, that partition was wrong. Our position was that America needed to intervene for any solution to be found, and that's exactly what happened. We succeeded in getting President Clinton involved –

President Clinton and George Mitchell. And I think everybody involved, unionists and everyone else, would agree that instead of admiring the problem, Americans attacked it, which is what they do. Without them there wouldn't be a peace process. So those who say we Irish-Americans don't understand, don't understand our history. Our history was founded on the worst genocide of the nineteenth century, which was the Irish Famine, and I think we've lived that history every day. I would never have gone to America if there hadn't been a famine. If there hadn't been the huge expulsion from Ireland, there wouldn't have been the Irish-American community. I think we understand very well.

The Centenaries

As a historical reality, the signing of the Ulster Covenant should be commemorated. But it always spoke to me of the hypocrisy of unionism, by saying that nationalists had to abide by political means, when 1912 was the very antithesis of all that. Because 1912 was the declaration of war against the Home Rule Bill, a declaration of war by unionism, which was followed up by the Curragh Mutiny, which was followed up by what occurred after the 1916 Rising. So from that point of view it's a very important moment in Irish history. It's not one that I think unionism should be particularly proud of, because it's a notion that democracy or the rule of law was secondary to their belief that they wanted to remain part of the United Kingdom. They were entitled to want that, but they literally took up arms right after the Covenant. And the fact that they took up arms led to, in many ways, the Easter Rising.

Yes, they had prime ministers and opposition ministers on their side. But the latest revelations from Cabinet papers reveal that Britain had interests beyond taking sides. What they were interested in at that point, the likes of Bonar Law and these people, was creating power for themselves. And with unionists, the Orange card was the one to play, to drive out Asquith and the Home Rule Bills. In other words, Ireland was a pawn of Britain's internal politics. I think unionism has learnt that lesson as the years have gone by, that the British commitment to Northern Ireland is very tenuous. Even Margaret Thatcher was openly discussing pulling out of Northern Ireland, which came as a shock to me personally, to be honest.

They have a point; the vast majority of the unionist population felt very strongly about Home Rule. But equally, the 1918 election was a huge endorsement of nationalism on the island of Ireland, where 78 per cent of the Irish people voted for some form of Irish unification. So from that point of view, you had two separate arguments, and those arguments should have been settled politically but they were settled militarily, unfortunately, with the creation of a completely artificial entity called Northern Ireland, which was essentially roped off from the rest of Ireland and made a Protestant state for a Protestant people. That was not the correct resolution of that argument at all.

I think the signing of the Covenant should be commemorated as that – as a historical event. It's like the outbreak of the First World War; people have to understand why the First World War started, even though it's incredibly obscure in many ways, and how every nation suddenly became involved in this horrific conflict. The origins of the Northern Ireland conflict are a lot clearer. It starts in 1912, fundamentally, with this declaration that by hook or by crook, we would never join Home Rule or a united Ireland of any kind. We will fight, we will use military force. And that was throwing down the Orange card. Then of course right away the Green card was thrown down, saying, 'Well if that's the way it is, that's the way it's going to be.'

I think a fitting commemoration would be an acknowledgement that half a million or so unionists came together and said, 'We are going to fight for our right to remain British.' That is a historical fact. I certainly wouldn't celebrate it, and I certainly wouldn't promote it, but I think it's obviously a historical reality that needs to be related to and acknowledged in that context, as a historical reality. I'm sure unionists are proud of it; it was their way of standing up and speaking out. But they can't use the double argument that somehow, subsequently, violence was used to make a point when it should have been politics, because they began the roundabout, so to speak, and 1912 was the moment when that became clear.

I don't see any reason for nationalists to celebrate 1912 at all. I certainly think they can commemorate it, but I don't think it has anything to do with nationalism; it had to do with unionism. I'm not one of these characters who thinks we can all be 'Kumbaya', and sit down and agree on everyone's history. The reality is that the signing was a very sectarian event. I'm sure unionists would not want to celebrate the 1916 Rising. I fully understand that as well. I'm not going to be brought into this notion that just because the Queen came to Ireland, all our history flows together in one seamless current. It's not like that. Bad things happened; very bad things happened as a result of 1912. The partition of Ireland was one of the greatest destructive mistakes in the history of Ireland, when unionists refused to accept the will of the majority. So I don't think nationalism has anything to celebrate at all.

I can see the argument that the First World War should be remembered by nationalists as well as unionists, because many nationalists gave their lives, they joined the British Army, and nationalists never fully understood or conceded that those people were doing what they thought was right. That was fair enough. But I do not see the same reality with the 1912 Covenant. I see that as a sectarian celebration of something that had only bad consequences. So be it. That's what history teaches us. We're not all going to celebrate Hitler's rise to power in Germany either [*Laughs*].

A lot of this stuff is political correctness and I don't agree with it. I find it disgusting that we're somehow supposed to celebrate, you know, the Orange marches on 12 July. Good luck to the Orangemen for celebrating those things. That's their history and tradition – it's not a nationalist tradition. It's a bit like me saying I'm going to go out on Puerto Rican Day instead of St Patrick's Day. That's not my day and that's just a reality.

Don't get me wrong. I have a great sense of what Ian Paisley did, what Peter Robinson did, what David Trimble did. Those were magnificent leaders who led their people, however slowly or cautiously, out of the cul-de-sac in which they had ended up. I had tremendous admiration for them. But I do not have admiration for people who turn to the gun at the first sign that they weren't going to get their way. That never has been and never will be the way I feel about that. I would see it in the context of a historical reality, where unionists may well want to celebrate that they became utterly recalcitrant on the subject of whether there should be a united Ireland. And no, I don't think there should be a military element to the commemoration of 1912. I would celebrate it very quietly if I was them. I don't think there's a lot to be proud of. I'm not going to celebrate the murders carried out on the nationalist side either. And I'm not going to celebrate some of the dreadful killings of Protestants that occurred around the 1798 Rising.

Nor do I see why any nationalist or republican should attend a 1912 ceremony. There's nothing there for them but the contempt that was delivered in 1912, saying your point of view doesn't matter. I think republicans should have gone to meet the Queen. I think they should have done a lot of things they didn't do. But I think 1912 was a sectarian outburst which created massive problems and cost tens of thousands of deaths in this country.

Easter 1916, on the other hand, I see that as the cornerstone of the Irish state. I see the 1916 Proclamation as the foundation document. It's hugely important in terms of Irish identity, not just in Ireland but worldwide. It was the fire that lit the inspiration for millions of Irish-Americans, Irish-Australians, Irish-Canadians, as they suddenly realised the Irish were going to step forward and take their place among the nations of the world. I would commemorate it the same way I would commemorate the American Declaration of Independence in America. It's a foundation document that gets more and more important as the years go on. I think the hundredth anniversary is a huge event for nationalists to celebrate.

I think you would disguise the face of history if you didn't commemorate it as a military event. It was a military defeat, there's no question about that. It's classically Irish, our revolution. It's not like the American one. We didn't win, but we won by losing [*Laughs*]. Again, the reality of it is that this Irish state would not exist without 1916, and I think I have always looked on them as heroic figures and I will continue to do so, and anyone who looks on them otherwise is misunderstanding the bravery and the incredible courage of going out, knowing you were going to be killed, in pursuit of an ideal. Some people may consider it madness and it may well have been. But it happened. It's the madness of George Washington taking on the British Army; it's the madness of the French Revolution; it's the madness of Egypt when they went to Tahrir Square. That's how revolutions begin. I was in India, speaking to people there, and the inspiration of the Irish uprising was very real for them, when they began their battle against the British.

If you look at Northern Ireland, it had a very passive history on the nationalist side for fifty years. The old nationalist party basically got kicked around by the unionists, got nothing. Then a younger generation came up – something like Tahrir Square – and they said, 'We've had enough of this', and they spoke up. That's what that was about – that was nothing to do with 1916, even though in the historical continuum, 1916 is linked to what happened in Northern Ireland. But 1966's commemoration had absolutely nothing to do with John Hume taking to the streets, or Austin Currie or anyone else talking about 'We Shall Overcome' a year or two later. Yes, there were decades of violence, but John Hume and the people who led the civil rights movement, they talk much more about Martin Luther King than 1916. That was their inspiration originally – people who didn't have 'one man, one vote', or who didn't have a single representative bar one in fifty years. I mean those were huge, massive civil rights outrages that were being carried out by the Protestant state against the Catholic people.

I remember the fiftieth anniversary of 1916 very clearly: they had the re-enactment of what happened. And I remember an interview with the sister of James Connolly. I never realised what Connolly went through. These were scholars, poets – extraordinary people in their own way. William Butler Yeats, I think, caught it best with the 'terrible beauty' poem. The fact that they went forth at that time was very inspiring to me then. What was I … thirteen years old at the time? It did have an impact on me, but I was very proud of it and remain very proud of it.

I don't think there are dangers in its commemoration. I don't find a commemoration of the American Revolution anything other than inspiring. I don't find a commemoration of the 1798 Rising anything but inspiring. I think these were people who stood up for the rights of man – the rights of people, as Thomas Paine would put it – and I think the 1916 Rising, with the combination of people who took part in it, was exactly the same.

Will it create division? The unionists are not shrinking violets. The unionists, to be fair to them, have moved so far, so fast, in their own way in the last fifteen years, I have great admiration for unionist leadership. I never thought I'd say that about Ian Paisley and I never thought I'd say that about David Trimble, both of whom I've met and had many discussions with, but I do. And they have moved forward; they understand the difference between a commemoration and something that inspires more violence. I think the commemoration of 1916 is hugely important on a global stage for Ireland – that we took our place among the nations of the earth. And again, it was a culmination of a history, a very proud history of Irish rebellion against the British. Yes, I'm sure it will raise the issue of partition, but you know, the issue has been settled for my lifetime and the lifetime of my offspring. What's happened in the north is John Hume's concept of an agreed Ireland. There is an Agreement now, that nationalists are no longer the people held down, that they have equal rights in government and that they have equal rights of representation. The unionists have accepted the need for power-sharing; they've accepted the need for equality, basically, which is what the 1968 protestors were talking about. So I think for my generation, I would prefer to see that than somebody coerced into something, which is what happened with partition to begin with.

Certainly in 1916 they used military means. But military means against the British Army is different from military means against a population that wasn't armed, which is what happened in the north, where this arbitrary border was drawn. It was always, living in County Louth, a fascination to me: where was that moment or where was that line or where was that road that was suddenly in the south when it used to be in the north? I mean it was an insane border. There was no natural geographic entity that made it a border. The greatest mistake of the last hundred years was partition, not the 1916 Rising.

I personally would love to see a united Ireland. I think this country has been stymied because of the lack of unity. The Irish Republic has suffered greatly as the result of a sort of 'Little Ireland' mentality that Northern Ireland wasn't part of this island for sixty, seventy years, and I think that, historically, partition will be seen as the greatest mistake by the British, as it was in India and in any other country they partitioned. It doesn't work. It doesn't work as a long-term solution to anything, and it didn't work in Ireland. Fortunately, through the efforts of some great people, the reality now is that there's an acceptance of the status quo in the north and in the south, an acceptance of an agreed Ireland, which is what I would look for. I think at this moment in time, if there was a referendum on Irish unification, the majority of people in the north would not vote for it, and that's a reality I have to accept. Retrospectively, if you look at the 1916 Rising, it wasn't about a mandate for constitutional change [*Laughs*]. It was about a mandate for revolution, and that's a very different thing. And by 1918, people had voted for that revolution.

History is a messy business, I think it is incomplete and I think it'll be incomplete for our lifetime. What I'm most proud of is that I'm not waking up every morning, turning on RTÉ, and hearing that two more bodies were found wherever, or somebody was blown up. I think for our generation, in our time, to have accomplished what we did, which was to end what was a very, very … I mean, if you look at the numbers killed on the American scale, it would have been 70,000 Americans killed in the thirty years of the Troubles. Those are massive figures; they had massive impact on people's lives. And I've met enough of the victims to know that getting beyond the violence and into politics was a huge singular achievement by the people of this generation.

I think we're nearer to achieving the aims of Easter 1916 than we were forty years ago. I do. Because I think we can make a convincing argument, as we did to Ian Paisley and David Trimble, that we can work together. Somewhere down the road it may even be in their interests to think about Britain's clear lack of interest in them, to realise that they've far more friends in the Irish Republic than they do in Britain. I think that that is now on the table for discussion at some point. You know, people in Ireland are very rooted in the idea that things don't change. If you'd told me fifteen years ago that Martin McGuinness and Ian Paisley would be in government together, I'd have suggested a good psychiatrist. And that's the reality – things are changing and changing dramatically, so suddenly things are on the table again, and I think that's fair enough.

As far as the First World War is concerned, my thoughts are that it was an absolutely catastrophic event that should never have happened; that thousands and thousands of Irish people – Northern Irish Protestants and Irish Catholics – died needlessly. I had occasion to meet someone in New York who was from Newfoundland and was in an Irish organisation there, and he was telling me they lost, I think it was 800 men on day one of the Battle of the Somme. They were all Irish-Canadian kids who died. It was a war that made no sense. Everybody can see what the Second World War was about – it was good versus evil in its clearest form. The First World War was a complete disaster and the Battle of the Somme was a complete disaster.

So I very much side with those who say there was absolutely no sense to what happened at the Somme, on either side. I see a case for retroactively court-martialling the British Army Chief-of-Staff, General Haig [*Laughs*]. That's what I see. And all his men who led the soldiers across no man's land. I don't know how many died, but hundreds of thousands died for three-and-a-half miles of land. It was an insane battle. The courage and the bravery of the men who died should be remembered because they were the cannon fodder. They lived in a very different era, where men were sent forth to die so that generals could draw lines on maps. Those ordinary soldiers, absolutely; but the notion of glorifying what the Somme really was about would be a huge mistake.

I do see an opportunity for getting together on this one. I see that the Ulster Volunteer Force and the Irish side could come together and say, 'Look, they were heroes.' You know the great phrase 'They were lions led by donkeys' – absolutely true. On both sides, the men of Northern Ireland and the men of the Irish Republic who fell in that war should be commemorated together.

There are dangers and opportunities in these centenaries. The danger of misinterpreting history in Irish terms is very real; that you somehow elide over what were actually very serious and very negative developments. The 1912 signing of the Covenant led to a host of militaristic realities that live with us to the present day. The signing of the Covenant was the first warning shot.

I think the opportunity is to realise that the Easter Rising was the foundation stone of the Irish state. It's something we need to get back to, the ideals which those men stood for, as against what we see today, which is endless corruption. They created a society that became an independent country effectively in 1921, but for ninety years that country has been mismanaged economically. We've had maybe ten years of good government, and every thirty years we've had this huge surge of emigration – the 1930s, the '50s, the '90s, and now again the '80s and 2010s. We need to go back to what those men were saying. The Proclamation is a wonderful document. It's something that was ahead of its time and I revere it as a document, almost to the extent that it stands beside what Jefferson wrote in the Declaration of Independence.

But I don't think these centenaries will create division, I think we've moved on and we see them in the proper historical context. If the Troubles in the north were still ongoing, I would say definitely yes, these two events could be seen as perpetuating or the continuing the division. But we've moved on, with the Good Friday Agreement, the power-sharing government, the intervention of the United States, the intervention of the Irish and British Governments, the extraordinary achievement of the Irish peace process. When history is written, this era will be remembered as a golden era, even though we may not think so, because of what was accomplished by the Irish peace process, which ended the longest-running warfare in Europe, and which has become the defining example of how things could happen elsewhere in the world. It's something we should be very proud of. And I think it overcomes that sectarian aspect of 1916 or 1921 enough that people can look at these from the perspective of history. What we all want is for the Battle of the Boyne to be a historical event, not an event that influences violence today. And it's the same with 1912 and 1916. For me, 1916 is a particularly proud moment, the proudest moment in the history of the Irish, where they stood forth in front of the world and proclaimed our new nation.

DAVY ADAMS

Davy Adams was a leading figure in the loyalist paramilitary group the Ulster Defence Association (UDA). He helped bring about the loyalist ceasefire in 1994 and ran as an Assembly candidate in 1998 but failed to be elected. He currently works for the Irish aid agency GOAL and is a columnist with The Irish Times.

Background

Politics were definitely not discussed when we were growing up. I mean, the only time it became an issue of discussion was when the civil rights movement started, and from that the Troubles. Growing up, we were so poor that the whole struggle – and it was an absolute struggle – was just to put food on the table. I was one of ten children and that was the everyday worry – just surviving and getting the money to survive and to do the best you could for your family.

But I did grow up in a very unionist home. I mean, my mother would never have told you who to vote for and would have made a point of that, but you absorb the politics of your own home. She insisted that we always voted because she said it was the one time everyone was equal. So I sort of absorbed unionism without having it preached or lectured to me. We were the only Protestants in our small row of houses but it was very much a predominantly unionist area. Three-quarters of the population could have sat at home and the unionist guy would still have swept home with the vote. But everybody went out to vote because it was just the thing to do.

My thinking changed as the Troubles deepened. My parents always had a major fear that any of us would become involved with or enthralled by Paisley or any of his people, but they never really had much of a fear we'd become involved in paramilitarism because they thought we were all too sensible. They were wrong in my case, but I was the only one. I joined the UDA. To be honest, there was a real resentment amongst working-class people of the unionist persuasion who were being lectured all the time about how deprived people were. I mean, we had nothing either, and it was as if we were living in the lap of luxury. And then you would know people who were killed, people who were in no-warning bombs or shot on the least excuse, or no excuse at all. [*Sighs*] This isn't an excuse, because there isn't any excuse, but your moral boundaries sort of shift and you never see an end to the Troubles. It's quite easy if you're the sort that hasn't a lot of common sense, to be honest and frank in my own case; it's quite easy to be attracted to easy solutions. You think there's going to be no end to the Troubles, so moral boundaries shift.

I joined the UDA very late, in relative terms – I would have been in my early twenties – and it flowed from knowing people who had been murdered and decent people who had done no one any wrong. Against that, I was raised in a very anti-sectarian home. So I suppose you could say that I eventually found my way back to where I should have been. You're attracted into these things and you can make all sorts of excuses, but I often think to myself that for every young person who joined the IRA or the UDA or the UVF, there were ten or twenty who had the sense not to.

These days, my thinking is massively changed. In fact, I'm not even sure that I would have a party political mode of thinking. I would be unionist because I happen to think that's where the best future lies. According to the Good Friday Agreement, and I stick very much by that, if the majority on both sides of the border voted for a united Ireland, they would get no reaction from me. But I think in real terms – and I've said it in my columns, so this is nothing new – if there was a proper united Ireland out there, that would benefit us all and suit us all, where the pain and hatred and nastiness could be set aside or left behind, that would be no problem for me.

The Centenaries

This may be wishful thinking [*Laughs*], but I think that if there's a balance to be found between the three centenaries, and people can reach sort of side-bar agreements with each other, they can be celebrated without offence to anyone, without offence being taken by anyone, without allowing old wounds to be opened and old pains to be resurrected, and the war by other means started again. I know the Assembly up there aren't doing much in real terms, but I think they're doing an awful lot in terms of building understandings and building relationships, not only among themselves, but ones that bleed down into the wider community. So I'm hoping that will extend to how we handle the three anniversaries. And I believe it will, because it's in the interests of everyone. It used to be in the interests of major parties to keep the conflict going. I think it's now in their interests to do the opposite. I think and hope and pray that they will work behind the scenes to get something smoothed out. I know it's an old cliché but we really can't deny history. However, I think there's a difference between not denying it and wallowing in it and being selective about it, and elevating the historic events, whether you agree with them or not, above others. I think we can find a balance. I mean, good God, we're bound to be mature enough now to find some kind of balance and some way to handle it, and now is the time to be start thinking about those things.

A bad way of commemorating would be if it was too militaristic; if it was about getting one over on the other community, about celebrating subjugation, instead of pointing out that unionism should always have been about everyone. There are no more multi-racial, multi-ethnic, multi-religious communities than there are within the UK. That's what unionism should have been pointing out for years and should be pointing out. So a bad commemoration would be singular, it would be triumphalist, it would be about subjugation, it would be harking back to supposed good old days, when unionists ruled the roost completely – that, to me, would be a bad commemoration.

It's all about attitudes as well. It's about the attitudes of those in television, far more than what people say in the press, for example. People have to set the right tone at the beginning of this, and start talking about inclusivity and about the union and how good it has been and can be, but also about the problems, the mistakes that were made, and how there wasn't much effort at all put into trying to be inclusive and selling the union the way it should be. Anyone from Northern Ireland knows it's not terribly difficult to sell something in a bad way. You've just got to set a bad tone. And people do take, on both sides of the community, the lowest common denominator as representative of the broader field.

Republicans being invited? I think there's more chance of them being invited to the signing of the Covenant commemorations than there is of them going [*Laughs*]. I would love to see them accepting an invitation, and it certainly would set a tone. I think if there's a quiet signal sent that it would be a good, decent thing to do, that it would be an intelligent thing to do, to invite republicans, then I don't see a problem with that. Things can change. There are still issues around, for example, the refusal of the Lord Mayor to present the Duke of Edinburgh medal to a young fifteen-year-old girl. I mean, people described it as bigotry and all the rest of it; I just thought of it as absolute stupidity. There wouldn't have been a word about it; no one would have even noticed. So I hope I'm wrong but I am just not too optimistic on that front. It would be great if people from all sections took part in each of the commemorations, but even if that doesn't happen, I don't think that's a recipe for disaster necessarily. I think it can still be handled.

I do think it's an opportunity for unionists to reflect on unionism, to some extent. But no one can say that unionism hasn't spent forty years reflecting on unionism. An awful lot of it had to be forced on them, but it happened none the less. I think there needs to be a bit of reflection on what people believed their political ideology to have been and what the reality of it was.

As for the Easter 1916 commemorations in Dublin and across the Republic, I'm not certain how it'll happen. There'll be all sorts of celebrations and dignitaries and parades and all the rest of it, and you would expect that. I dare say there will be some replication of that in some areas in Northern Ireland. But so what? We're well used with commemorations and parades. It's the speeches that are made at these parades; it's what's on show and who's being deified.

Of course there'll be television coverage of all of this. I was lucky enough, going to grammar school, to have studied Irish history extensively, so there was never anything there that I didn't know about or was at least taught about – whether I remember it or not is another question [*Laughs*]. But there's widespread ignorance in the unionist community about 1916, and a few television programmes about it would do no harm. But again, it's about how they're handled, how they're presented. You'd like to think that the more responsible sections of our media in Northern Ireland would be alive to the potential problems that can be created.

We all know how programmes can be deliberately slanted. Without being able to put your finger on the points, exactly, you know you can feel the slant of programmes. What we need is a straight historical piece – or two or three – on the Easter Rising; what foreshadowed it, what brought it about, what followed, the Civil War even. And you know, the state that came from it wasn't exactly in line with Irish republicanism – I would argue it wasn't within a beagle's goul of Irish republicanism. But maybe that's going too far, for that's slanting it in another direction. So I mean just a straight historical piece is required.

There's an argument for a unionist-style commemoration of the signing of the Covenant, balanced by a republican-style commemoration of Easter 1916, but it's not one that I, in this context, would go along with. I think what's needed is a straight historical description of what happened and why. I wonder if sometimes taking this idea of balance is wandering off the subject a little bit, almost to the extreme where no matter how unrepresentative, we feel we have to have every voice throwing their tuppenceworth in, just so we can walk away and say, 'That's balanced, you know.' I mean, what's wrong with straight historical reporting of what happened?

The part played by television will be important. For an awful lot of people, reading isn't quite the activity it once was – far from it, in fact. Some of us read newspapers, but the quality newspapers aren't as heavy on the ground as they once were. Television has a massive influence on everything. We can talk about the internet, and it does have impact to a certain extent, but television is the thing. It's no accident that when some group takes over a country, the first place they try to take is the television station.

There's a great opportunity here as well and I think that we shouldn't concentrate too much on the pitfalls and the possible problems. There is a great opportunity for education here and about understanding other points of view – about realising how people got to the position they were in, how people ended up with their beliefs and allegiances, and how people who have different allegiances don't necessarily have to be enemies, even such starkly different allegiances as those to an Irish Republic or those to a Northern Ireland within the United Kingdom. There's a real opportunity for historical understanding and for people to realise that things do not happen in a vacuum. There's a backdrop to everything, and the more you understand the backdrop, the more you understand how things happened and the more you understand, hopefully, similar things happening in the future. There's nothing to be feared from a two-eyed presentation of history, but there's everything to be lost if you go down the road again of presenting this one-eyed view for unionists and then a one-eyed view for republicans, and then sitting back and thinking you've done your job. You actually haven't. What you've done is you've fed the lowest common denominator on one side, and entrenched them, creating no sense of understanding at all, and then you have done the same for the other side. That to me isn't balanced. There is an argument that it's not the role of television to create understanding, but against that it is the role, at least of the BBC, to be fair and balanced. So each programme should be a historical analysis, a straight historical analysis pointing out benefits, faults, why people made the decisions they did and all the rest of it.

Today's unionists probably do have a lot to learn from study of the signing of the Covenant, because their history doesn't go back far enough. I'm not suggesting they go back until the time itself, but to think of unionism beyond their own experience of it. There is stuff to be learnt there. And I think it's the same with republicanism. I actually think 1916 isn't the greatest place to start if you want to learn anything about actual Irish republicanism, as opposed to the imposters. Republicanism can mean anything, but Irish republicanism as described by Wolfe Tone and Henry Joy McCracken and those people – all of that was lost. And I don't think 1916 necessarily represented republicanism. It represented nationalism – a republic came later. If all of the leaders of 1916 had survived, I'm not sure how long they would have got along together [*Laughs*].

Unionists could benefit from reflecting on 1916, if it's pitched in the right way; if it's not pitched in the sense of, 'they're totally in the wrong and they're stupid, or pig-headed or blind to where their real interests lie,' and all the rest of it. What unionism has to learn and what republicanism has to learn is Irishness – the breadth of Irishness. It doesn't stop at a certain religion or a certain set of political views, and it never did until relatively recent times. My father was born before partition, and a lot of his modes of reference were in an Irish content. He'd say, 'Ah, you wouldn't meet a dafter man if you walked to Dublin!' And if you'd asked him if he was Irish he'd have laughed at you. 'Do you think I'm Australian or something?' That was lost, so we all have to learn that Irishness doesn't belong to one, almost singular identity.

It's probably dreaming too much about what could be achieved, but it's more about putting yourself in the other person's shoes at that time. And I think it can happen. I think it's not an either/or situation. In some cases it may happen and in some cases it will happen. They'll say, 'Oh jeez, now I understand. I mightn't agree but I can understand why they did that.'

Of course there's a massive danger that the centenaries will deepen entrenchment. But the flip-side is, the only way to avoid any danger is to ignore them altogether, and that's impossible, we just can't do that. So we move to the next position, which is to try to manage them, doing as little damage as possible. Then you become a little more ambitious and you say, 'Why not actually use these? Why not go for some form of building bridges, of educating each other, of feeling more comfortable with each other, to create a bit of understanding, at least of how people ended up doing things?'

It's hard even now for people to put themselves back into the 1950s, to situations where we grew up in absolute poverty, not knowing where the next shilling was coming from, so it's a bit of a task to take them back further still, to not only the social situation but the political situation, and how people felt at that time. But it's not impossible. I think we underestimate ourselves far, far too much in Northern Ireland. We just say, 'Ah Jesus, we can't trust ourselves to do this, that or the other.' And often, almost subconsciously, you can attract the reaction that you expect – not that you want but that you expect. Instead, why not go for it? Let's go for it and do it properly, and do it hoping for the best and planning to get the best from both sides of the community.

I think Easter 1916 is likely to be commemorated far differently in the north than in the south. The problem, and it's wholly understandable, is that republicans and nationalists go overboard in the north to prove how Irish and republican they are [*Laughs*]. Whereas down here in the south, they're far more relaxed about it. I think the commemoration will be a relaxed thing here – probably far, far better done in terms of presenting different sides of the story accurately.

It's understandable that Northern unionists are going to be more British than the British, and Northern nationalists and republicans are going to be more Irish than the Irish. I'm not sure how far that'll go but I think you'll see a distinct difference. Down here an awful lot of it will be officially organised by wise heads and people who are not going to score politically. Fine Gael and Fianna Fáil aren't going to score political points off each other through the political commemorations. I think the Shinners are always caught between trying to build bridges and trying to solidify their position politically. But then what political party isn't? So I'm not sure how they'll approach it. But you know, I just don't think it'll be as sensible up north as it'll be down here [*Laughs*].

Commemoration of the Battle of the Somme will be a different kind of centenary. The 36th Ulster Division and the Irish Division fought side by side. There's no difference in how they looked at each other or how they felt, they were comrades in arms. It was a sacrifice made by people from all arts and parts of Ireland, and from all religions and all politics, so I think it has real potential for being commemorated in the proper sense and it has far more legitimacy for being commemorated right across the communities. Unionism has tended to hold it as a purely unionist event, although that also has something to do with nationalism tending to take it and shove it away. It never was and it never should have been treated like that.

I see a change, though, down here in the south at least. I've seen people here in Dún Laoghaire – though not very many – with the poppy. I saw them last year as well. President McAleese and her husband had an awful lot to do with that sort of thing. That's what I mean when I'm talking about history – looking at it through both eyes as opposed to one. A lot of those families who were denied and who, for one reason or another, couldn't commemorate their parents' or grandparents' part in the First World War – it's changing for them as well. And I think it's seeping up North.

It was an imperial war – I think that should and will be emphasised. Whether it will be in Northern Ireland or not, I don't know. But in general – and in UK commemorations on Remembrance Day – the futility of it is always raised, particularly in terms of the First World War. You know the old one, 'Lions led by donkeys'. It wasn't quite the case but that certainly has got a grip now on people's understanding of that event.

I'm an optimist about these centenaries generally. What we haven't realised for a long time, and I knew this raising my own children, is that there have been young people mixing in bars and clubs for years. All we could see was the other section of youth, at barricades and rioting, and all the rest of it. There's a whole stratum of young people who've been mixing, and that's gradually growing. I see it even in the place where I live. I think both communities in Northern Ireland are so wary of allowing ourselves to be tempted or drawn or nudged back into anything like the past that we're willing to stretch a bit.

And minds are broadening – I've no doubt about that. You've only to look at who's sitting up in Stormont together. That has set a great example to the rest of Northern Ireland. I think sometimes we become so wary and so scared of things – our fears and prophecies – it's almost self-fulfilling. I'm optimistic that things can pass off okay. Seize the opportunity. I mean, we can't deny these events – that would be the worst thing to do. The next worst thing would be to be sort of half-hearted. They're going to happen, they're historical events, let's look at them, let's commemorate them. And let's try and do it in as reasonable and as sensible a manner possible, with an underlying notion of using them to help better understanding across communities.

OWEN PATERSON

Owen Paterson has been the MP for North Shropshire since 1997. He was appointed Shadow Secretary of State for Northern Ireland in 2007 and has been Secretary of State for Northern Ireland since 2010. He is a strong supporter of the Royal Irish Regiment (RIR), which is based in his constituency.

Background

When I was at Cambridge we talked about politics, but I wasn't involved in student politics at all. Locally was how I got involved, in a charity project very near to my home – a cottage hospital. Bizarrely I ended up buying it, and set up a trust to run it. And there was another charity project I got involved in, a project to set up an arthritis research centre.

But I used to travel a huge amount. I think I went to something like sixty or seventy countries through the 1980 and '90s, and I saw how some countries were a lot better run than others. I grew up with the Soviet Union, and when the Wall came down I went over it – actually just before it came down, we did quite a lot of business – and I saw the horrendous damage caused by the Soviet Union, not just in what is now Russia but all across Eastern Europe. I went to China a few weeks after the Gang of Four fell. It's quite impressive, at the age of seventeen, to see someone pursued up the street by a policeman with a fixed bayonet! So I had clear views on a free society and totalitarian systems.

I've been coming here to Northern Ireland pretty well every week since David Cameron asked me to be the Shadow [Secretary of State for Northern Ireland] in July 2007. And because most of the devolution legislation had gone through, I made a real point of coming here on a weekly basis – if I missed a week I'd double up the following week. I've also been the Secretary of State since the last elections, so that's nearly coming up for five years. I think I see things here from both angles. I mean, I represent North Shropshire, which is a very solid English seat, but I've been in parliament since 1997. I think David Cameron is very sensible, and the way he leaves his Shadows to take on the real role has given me a great lift.

I met an awful lot of people here, and I spent a lot of time in Dublin as a Shadow, where I met members of all parties, who were very generous with their time. For example, Enda Kenny, when he was leader of the Opposition, always found time to see me. So I hope I've got quite a balanced view of things.

The Centenaries

I see these centenaries as a tremendous opportunity. We've been working very closely with various ministers in Dublin and talking to the Executive here for many months now. I think that if we can work together and set the tone of the narrative, these centenary celebrations could be really beneficial. However controversial and dramatic an event might have been at the time, it was a key part in getting to where we are now. By recognising it, you're not necessarily celebrating it, but are helping, I think, to educate people. There are, as we know, some fairly simplistic views of history. I think it's really important that each of these events is treated in a respectful manner and in a broadly educational manner, so that we all come out better informed.

I thought the couple of events we've done recently show how we can do this. First of all, the Taoiseach was over. He did a joint statement with the Prime Minister, but then he went pretty quickly afterwards to Westminster Hall, where we opened a small exhibition on the Home Rule Bill. From an English perspective, the Home Rule Bills – 1912 was the third one – dominated the politics of Westminster for decades, so I thought it was absolutely appropriate that we should have an exhibition on the history behind it, how the Third Home Rule Bill was introduced. The Taoiseach came along and took a real interest in it.

We were in Dublin last week, which I thought was very significant. Peter Robinson came down and delivered the Carson lecture, and I thought the way the Tánaiste introduced him and the way he spoke was really tremendous. It was in exactly the spirit of how we want this to go ahead. It was respectful but it was also educational. So we're talking about bringing the exhibition to Dublin next, and we've talked to Peter Robinson and Martin McGuinness and we may bring it to Stormont. I think that's an example of how we can work together.

I don't see the signing of the Ulster Covenant as a purely unionist event. I think it's really good that the government in Dublin have immediately gone ahead, in the centenary year of 1912, to show there were 30,000 Covenant signatures south of what is now the border. That is politically significant, and these events can be educational. It's probably not very widely known there were a significant number of signatures south of the border, and I think it is very good that, in a very measured way, the Republic has started a whole series of lectures – we had a genuine debate last week when Peter Robinson came down. Now I think it is also incumbent upon those who are strong supporters of the union here to celebrate – because they will be celebrating, we may as well recognise it – the Covenant in a measured way so it is, as I say, helpful to the narrative and educational, and not triumphalist.

The Covenant signing is one of the building blocks of history that has led to where we are. I was representing the British Government last week, and you had the Tánaiste, you had Peter Robinson, and everybody agreed that the current arrangements have put Ireland and the UK in a better position than they have been for decades. And we have massive endorsements through the referendums – 91 per cent and 71 per cent. Everyone agrees that the current arrangements are the best way forward and are settled. Therefore, all these building blocks, whether you like them or not, have got us to where we are. So I wouldn't expect republicans to be celebrating the signing of the Covenant but I thought they might participate and take an interest in what actually happened. They can learn from it; for example, the one little fact I mentioned – the 30,000 signatures.

What I'm keen on is that there is respect for what actually happened, and that there is a measure of education. If we have any doubts about centenaries, look at how the Queen and the President handled last year. That was potentially an immensely controversial centenary – the centenary of her grandfather's visit when he was the King. The way they both pulled it off is a lesson to us all. That's an example of a centenary which was potentially very divisive but actually turned out to be an enormously beneficial political event. I was in America for St Patrick's Day recently and they were still talking about it. It hasn't just moved on politics in the island of Ireland, it had moved on politics among Irish-Americans.

I don't think it's for me to lay down the law as to how commemorations are conducted [*Laughs*], but I think the way we've started, with a series of lectures, with exhibitions, with getting serious historians involved, possibly having stuff on websites, articles in the press – I think that's a good way forward. But as the summer moves on, we know there's going to be a big manifestation of some sort around the actual date, 28 September – it's going to happen on 29 September. I think this is all fine. But again the tone wants to be respectful, and again, I keep stressing this, it is helpful if it's educational. I think there is probably lots that people could learn.

I'm sure there's lots of information out there that could be more broadly disseminated which would be positive, which might change perceptions.

For republicans, the Easter Rising was a key event because it led to the establishment of what is now the Republic of Ireland. So I'm sure there will be all sorts of events in Dublin, which again I hope will be respectful and I hope will be educational. There may be commemoration north of the border, but I would have thought the main focus would be in Dublin, because that's where the Rising happened. If there are republicans in the north who want to commemorate 1916, they want to do it in a judicious, measured manner. It is very important and we are very keen, as the UK Government, working with the Republic of Ireland, working with the Executive here, not to have anything triumphalist or divisive. We want to be measured and reasonable. So in some cases you're going to recognise an event which was probably not in the interests of those of your background, but by recognising it you're not denying your own background. If there's something you're very much in favour of, again, you're bound to celebrate it, but again I say, don't do it in a manner which upsets your neighbours. Do it in a manner which perhaps educates your neighbours.

I don't see why there shouldn't be republicans in attendance at Covenant events and unionists in attendance at Easter Rising events. If we need an example of how to behave, look at what the Queen and the President did. The Queen at the Garden of Remembrance was a very major political event in its own right, and showed respect. In the last week at Iveagh House, you had Peter Robinson giving a lecture espousing the benefits of unionism. That was good. They invited him down there. I think that shows respect. And it was educational. All these events were stepping stones to where we are today. There's no point in anyone denying them and there's no point in anyone pretending they didn't happen. I think, go along in a respectful manner, absolutely.

I don't see why invitations shouldn't be extended to republicans or unionists, because there's no point denying that something happened. These things happened. We are where we are, and where we are is a massively better place than where we've been for decades.

For myself, I don't see why I wouldn't be in attendance at the Covenant commemoration in September. Likewise with Easter 2016 events. I think it'd be very odd if the British Government wasn't there. Look at how we've moved on, how we've moved beyond the peace process. We've got the

Taoiseach in Downing Street, working closely with David Cameron on a whole programme of stuff – economics, culture, sport, all these things we've got in common – because we're working so closely together.

As to the Battle of the Somme, well, I go to the Somme on 1 July every year, and I thought last year was really indicative of how we should handle it. When I was there, there was a minister from the Irish Government, and we went to Thiepval, which has the magnificent Lutyens Memorial to the Missing. Then went to the Ulster Tower, which celebrates the 36th division (the Ulster division), who fought on 1 July, but, very importantly, we then went to Guillemont, where the 16th Division fought with incredible bravery – men who were mainly recruited from what's now the Republic. And don't forget, every one of these Irishmen was a volunteer, which is an extraordinary fact – there was absolutely no conscription. After that we went to a Catholic church in Guillemont with all sorts of memorials, one of which was to three young Irishmen who got the Victoria Cross south of there. There I was, standing with the Irish minister and the Duke of Gloucester. And of course outside you had the band of the Royal Irish Regiment, whose wristband I have got on. They are based in my constituency and 20 per cent of their current force is from the south.

So I believe we should go along to these events, which are extraordinarily moving, remembering that every single one of the Irishmen who died or was horribly wounded during the Battle of the Somme was a volunteer, and every one of them was fighting to defend the freedom of people, not just across the British Isles but across the world. If there had been a German takeover there would have been a very unsatisfactory result.

The suggestion that any of these men enlisted for the sake of a job is completely bizarre, or that they went with anything but the motive that they were doing the right thing. They volunteered. There were 49,000 of them remembered at the other Lutyen's memorial at Islandbridge, which of course has been renovated. I went to Islandbridge probably thirty years ago, and it was sad, it was run-down, it was covered in graffiti. It's now been beautifully restored and it plays a key part in the life of the Republic of Ireland. Actually, Minister Brian Hayes told me last week that there is the possibility of a splendid plan to complete the Lutyens project, to build a bridge across the river, because since the Queen's visit they've had so many visitors. Now that I think shows exactly the progression we want to make.

These centenaries could be very divisive and could push people back into a simplistic view. Each of these events was very dramatic and is still controversial, but by celebrating or by recognising them in a respectful manner we will maintain a civilised narrative. The real goal now has to be a shared future, and we've been completely clear about this. The Prime Minister talked about this last year, when he came to Stormont, about a shared future, not a shared-out future. So these events led to the position we're in now, where we have the luxury – I mean, we're in the best position we've been in for decades – to help build a shared future. You build a shared future not by denying your own background or by denying someone else's, but by working with them and by acknowledging these events that got us to where we are. As governments, I'm not saying we're going to set the narrative, but I think we can help set the tone. If we don't do that, there is a danger these centenaries could be hijacked by people who do want to use them for their own very narrow objectives.

If they're handled correctly, they may well affect a change in public consciousness by the end of the decade of centenaries. If in doubt about any of this, look at how the Queen and the President of the Republic handled themselves last year, and look how they did change things. If we recognise events, and if we help educate people, we can show there are important steps to the position where we are today, where we can help build a shared future.

ROBERT BALLAGH

Robert Ballagh is an Irish artist, painter and designer, and is a member of Aosdána. His paintings are held in several public collections of Irish paintings, including the National Gallery of Ireland, the Hugh Lane Gallery, the Ulster Museum, Trinity College Dublin, and Nuremberg's Albrecht Dürer House.

Background

Politics were never discussed in my home, and much later on I discovered one of the possible reasons why. On my mother's side, during the Civil War, my grandmother and my grandfather were on opposite sides and ended up, I think, not talking for about a decade. So I can appreciate why my mother felt that politics was not a proper subject. In the case of my father, who came from a radically different background (my mother was a Roman Catholic, my father was a Presbyterian), he had no objection to talking about politics at all; but because his wife didn't talk about politics, certainly when I was a child, I didn't hear much discussion in the home. When I became older I would talk to him and we discussed politics quite a bit. He was what I would call an armchair socialist, an armchair republican. He never got involved in anything but his views would have been quite contrary to the class in which he found himself. He was a manager in a wholesale drapery in Dublin and I'm sure the management weren't too keen on socialism and things like that. He also was a very keen golfer and I would imagine that sitting at the bar in the golf club, going on about socialism and republicanism, wouldn't have gone down well with his fellow golfers.

It wasn't until I was a teenager that we discussed things. I think what I got from him more than anything was the notion of being a civic republican. I remember as a kid being amazed when one day I said, 'What are you doing?' and he said, 'I'm going in to see my pictures.' I said, 'What are you talking about?' And he said, 'I'm going into the National Gallery to see my pictures.' His attitude was that the National Gallery belonged to the people of Ireland and the pictures belonged to the people of Ireland, so they were his pictures. He loved parks and all those civic institutions that were part of the people's heritage. I think I learnt that from him – that sense of citizenship and that sense of civic pride in the things that belong communally to all of us.

I became interested in politics from the time I was in school. I became a doubter in terms of religious belief – a confused doubter but nevertheless a doubter – and at the same time became very concerned about social issues and about inequality in society. I was privileged to be sent to one of the 'better' schools in Dublin. I remember I got into trouble with some other boys at one stage. Believe it or not we were hauled up in front of the whole school – about a thousand pupils, it was a very big school – and were described as disgraceful and guilty of letting down the school. Our crime was to have talked to a group of girls at a football match! [*Laughs*] Believe it or not, in the 1950s that was a disgraceful thing to do. The thing I remember was that the president of the college, in criticising us, spoke to the whole college and said, 'You've got to understand, you boys, that you are going to become the future leaders of this society, and you have a responsibility to behave properly and give good example.' And I remember thinking at the time, 'Is he mad?' Because I was well aware that a lot of my school comrades were not the brightest; how in the name of goodness could he suggest that these were going to become the future leaders of society? He was right, of course [*Laughs*]. But I remember that made me think. Why is society constructed like this, where some people whose parents happen to have the desire or the money to send their children to a certain school can guarantee that their kids are going to run the country, whereas other parents who can't afford that and who have to send their kids to other schools, the Christian Brothers or something like that, they are going to be the drawers of water and the hewers of wood?

Nowadays, I would say I'm first of all a democrat. I believe in democracy. That's one of the reasons I'm profoundly depressed at the moment: I see in Ireland and Europe, but also across the world – our so-called Western World – an almost continual hollowing-out of democracy. We're given this charade of being allowed to vote every four or five years, but in between that crucial decisions are made, time and time again – in some cases going to war, in our case bailing out banks. Decisions on all of these issues that will impact not only on me but on my children and my grandchildren, and possibly their children as well, are made without any consultation with the people, or without taking into account the views of the people on these particular issues. That would be a great concern of mine.

I suppose I would also be a socialist, but I don't know how to define socialism nowadays. But if socialism means equality and justice for all, then I'm a socialist.

The Centenaries

The fiftieth anniversary of the Easter Rising didn't really have much effect on me, even though it was a fairly extensive affair. I know there are those who are critics of the armed struggle in the north who think the over-indulgent celebration in 1966 was what fuelled the Provos. I think that's absolute clap-trap. I don't think any of the people who became leading lights in the Provos sat through the four-hour pageant in Croke Park organised by my friend Tomás Mac Anna. There was also *Insurrection*, a TV drama done on a nightly basis portraying the events of Easter week, 1916. The interesting thing is it was written by Hugh Leonard, who later became a caustic critic of the nationalist struggle in the north. There's a certain irony there.

A lot of things happened between 1966, the fiftieth anniversary of Easter 1916, and 1991, the seventy-fifth anniversary. As we were approaching 1991 it became apparent that *nothing* was going to be done. The government was terribly reluctant, and I knew because of my involvement with stamp design over the years that they weren't even going to bring out a postage stamp to commemorate the seventy-fifth anniversary. I remember seeing something in the paper about a public meeting in Liberty Hall of concerned citizens about organising an adequate commemoration for the seventy-fifth anniversary of the Easter Rising, so I decided to go along. I think about 500 people turned up at Liberty Hall, and there was lively discussion. At the end they asked people to put their names forward for a committee or something. Then, lo and behold, I discovered I got elected – or nominated or whatever – onto the organising committee. I remember we had our first meeting and, to my huge surprise, I was elected chairman; so from being totally outside of it all, I suddenly found myself at its centre.

That was a really fascinating experience, because of the number of politicians and people who had decided that to commemorate this event in our history was tantamount to giving aid and comfort to the Provisional IRA. And no matter how you tried to argue that this was a historical, cultural commemoration, and it had nothing to do with support for an armed struggle or anything like that, it didn't dissuade those people. I mean, Des O'Malley spoke in the Dáil and said, 'Robert

Ballagh's committee is a propaganda tool for the Provisional IRA.' I was put under surveillance by the Special Branch.

It was a kind of crazy time. But the one thing that I am proud of is that this small committee of volunteers managed to put together a very adequate commemoration of the seventy-fifth anniversary, to the extent that at the last minute the government were embarrassed into putting on, I think, a rather pathetic fifteen-minute ceremony in O'Connell Street. But they wouldn't even have done that if we hadn't made the effort. Oh, and we also, by our pressure, reversed the government's decision not bring out a postage stamp.

As to the centenary of the signing of the Ulster Covenant, for a start I wouldn't use the word 'celebrate'. I never use that either about the Easter Rising. I think we commemorate these events; I don't like the notion of triumphalism or celebration. When they're going to commemorate the signing of the Ulster Covenant and all of that, I think it should be done in a sober, measured manner and not in any triumphalist way, because we do have a very conflicted and difficult history in this country, and the north has enough banging of drums and stuff like that. This should be done in a calm and measured way. An inflammatory way would be to have loads of marches and Lambeg drums, and all of that kind of thing. Parading into areas where they're not wanted – I think that would be completely unnecessary. Being an artist, I have in my mind that great image of Carson with the big round table and the Union Jack on it. It might be fun in the City Hall to restage that event; I think that might be interesting.

I'm conflicted, because at base I'm an anti-imperialist. And it's not my opinion; it's a fact that what they were engaged in was a pro-imperialist act. So I don't personally have a great deal of sympathy for this event. But I have to recognise that it is part of our joint history on this island, so I think it has to be commemorated in a sober and realistic manner. I wouldn't have a problem with attending if I'm invited, because in the recent past I've developed some strong friendships with people from the loyalist community – but I wouldn't be celebrating [*Laughs*].

The Somme and the First World War have a more universal context on the island, because I think up to 40,000 people from the south died in the First World War. For years I campaigned – more on an architectural front, but nevertheless – the fact that the memorial gardens in

Islandbridge lay more or less in disrepair for so long because of the conflicted history behind the whole Irish participation in the First World War. But the gardens are a favourite walk of mine – always were and continue to be. They were designed by Sir Edward Lutyens and they're a wonderful example of a contemplative, peaceful place. So I was delighted they were renovated and looked after, and that there were a lot of renovations and clean-ups for Her Majesty's visit.

But my feelings about the First World War? I believe it was a dreadful business entirely. It was an imperial war fought between imperial powers, and the working classes of all nations were sacrificed totally unnecessarily on the fields of Flanders, etc. It's only right and proper that all of those Irish people, north and south, who lost their lives in the First World War should be commemorated, and commemorated in the best way – not just for their courage. The people who went out there went out for myriad reasons. One of the things I remember – going back to art here – is Jim Plunkett's wonderful *Strumpet City*. The main character is a guy called Fitz, who's a socialist – a trade union shop steward in the gas company. When the trade unionists are defeated in the Lock-out they go back to work, and all his comrades in the gas company get their jobs back except him. He's blacklisted. He has a wife and children, and the only thing he can do is join the British Army. So he's not going out for King or Country; he's not going out there for some gallant cause or the stuff we heard about poor Belgium and the plight of small nations. And I think a lot of people, if they'd known how horrible it was going to be, wouldn't have volunteered. Of course in Britain they were conscripted, but in Ireland they were volunteers.

If I was doing anything I'd be laying a quiet personal flower at the memorial for all of these people. But I really do draw short from the poppies and all of that, because one of the things that repels me – and it's nothing to do with our joined history with Britain – is militarism of any shape or form. So much of the commemoration/celebration of that period is drenched in militarism and its symbols. I would definitely personally draw back from that.

How would I like Easter 1916 commemorated? Well, when we formed our committee in 1991 it was called, 'Reclaim the Spirit of Easter'. That was really what we were interested in. It's an exciting story, the story of the armed struggle of the volunteers in 1916, but I stressed all the time, and everyone on the committee agreed, that we weren't interested in commemorating the military struggle. We didn't see the seizing of the GPO as relevant to the situation that Ireland was in then and that Ireland is in now. We really believed that the dreams of those who got involved in 1916 were what was important, and were worth commemorating and remembering. I mean, Pearse's ideas on education – still radical today – haven't been fulfilled; James Connolly's notions on equality, social justice, etc., still haven't been realised. In fact, we went so far as to say that the reason why the authorities in 1991 were so unwilling to commemorate 1916 was that they would be shamed by the aims and dreams of those people. And I think it would be even more to the point now. Whatever little bit of independence and sovereignty we gained after the sacrifices of 1916, the present crowd have given away.

What the 1916 people had in mind was an independent thirty-two-county republic, there's no doubt about it. And I don't think they harboured any sectarian ideas at all in their aims and objectives. Unfortunately other things intervened. Connolly, for instance, said in a famous piece that if Ireland were partitioned it would cause a carnival of reaction, north and south, and I think he was right. We ended up creating on this island two sectarian states: one north and one south. There's always a lot of focus on the sectarian nature of the northern state, particularly in its first fifty-odd years. But, I mean, what about the state down here? The facts just keep coming out. I see there's a television series about to come out about how we incarcerated people in mental homes, how we incarcerated the children of the poor in institutions. And hovering over all of this was the Roman Catholic Church. So we did create two horrible states, north and south, as a consequence of the partitioning of this country.

Of course with commemorations there's always the danger of division, but a worse danger is to ignore everything. I think that you can ignore history. What is it, the famous phrase? Ignore your past and you're committed to repeating it – a bad paraphrase, but I think it's absolutely true. We've just got to be as careful as possible that in commemorating these events we try to avoid situations that will cause division. I think it is possible to do this, as long as, on both sides, we approach these historical events with some sensitivity and deal with them in a dignified and responsible manner.

I don't think there's a danger the other way, that the events will become insipid and colourless; especially talking about 1916, if you zero in on the aims and objectives and the dreams of those people, and don't spend so much time on the militaristic aspects. For instance, for the ninetieth anniversary, our government, because of the peace process, decided it was time to come out and do something, so we had the Irish Army in all its glory driving up and down O'Connell Street, and the few aeroplanes we have flying overhead. I was just kind of appalled by all of that. It's not that I've any prejudice against the Irish Army; I just said, 'This is not the way, you know.'

I believe the centenaries will mean a deepening of opposing identities. I think that's inevitable, that's a consequence of our history. But I think people have the right to express their deep convictions about what they believe, and if that's on one side nationalists and one side unionists, that's what we've got to deal with. Both sides just have to appreciate the complexities and the subtleties of these situations.

And yes, there's always the danger of being tethered to our past, but I do think there is relevance in looking at the 1916 period. I gave a paper a while ago where I tried to look at that period; not just 1916 but the last few decades of the nineteenth century, where you had the co-operative movement, the GAA, the foundation of the Abbey Theatre. All of these things to some extent culminated in 1916 and that period. They talk about the Irish revival, etc., and so much of that is relevant today. Not the militaristic aspects of it, but Connolly's ideas about equality and justice and fairness in our society – they are as relevant to somebody living on the Shankill Road as to someone living on the Falls Road. Pádraig Pearse's ideas of a decent education for all our children, which would inspire them creatively; what he wrote about that in his book *The Murder Machine* is as relevant today for Catholic children or Protestant children or the children of Dissenters. So I think we can celebrate all that stuff, without division.

At one stage the 1916 rebellion was nicknamed 'The Poets' Rebellion'. These weren't guerrilla fighters. One or two of them had experience in the British Army, but by and large they were teachers, they were poets, they were writers – Eamonn Ceannt played the uilleann pipes – and that's why I think they were interesting. They were people who had the imagination and vision to do something for their society. I think Ireland is crying out for that at the moment – people of vision and imagination. So it shouldn't be divisive to look at what these people believed in and what they wished for Ireland.

We know that in all this debate there are trigger words that drive certain people mad and comfort other people. I try desperately to find other words. I was asked to talk some time ago on a united Ireland or something like that, and I said, 'Well, could we not call it an agreed Ireland or something?' Because these are phrases that people are just repelled by, if they're from one sector, without thinking about what we're talking about. One of the things that seems almost self-evident to me is that, north and south, whether we like it or not, we're being driven together by what's happening in the world, what's happening in Europe, the economic situation. Leaving aside our historical baggage, our political baggage, it makes eminent sense to have some kind of all-Ireland economy. The notion of two different corporate tax rates north and south – what's that all about? That's just stupid. Why do we have two departments of health, two departments of education, two departments of social welfare, two departments of everything? Leaving aside politics, wouldn't it make so much more sense for us all to work together for the common benefit on this island?

I would like to think that artists like myself have something in particular to contribute to the commemoration of 1916. On a simply practical level, to be asked to do certain things, physical manifestations, whether they be, with our writers, with our actors staging dramatic events … I don't know if that's part of the scheme. That's what they did in 1966. They had several major exhibitions of artists' work. Hopefully for the centenary they would be done with some imagination and some vision.

One of the things I find about Ireland today is that there's a stultifying lack of imagination and vision. What artists bring, I think, if they're good and if they're genuine, is a different way of thinking. And Ireland is crying out for a different way of thinking about things. I can't be prescriptive about that, but one of the things I feel about political life in Ireland, north and south pretty much, is that it's like a train on tracks, and it just keeps going. Nobody is saying, 'Hold on a second, there's another way of doing this!' I mean, we in the south are completely hamstrung now because the government has signed us up to this EU/IMF deal, so effectively our politicians are carrying out what our European and international masters tell them to do. And we've got ourselves into this situation, where we are being led by people who are actually being led by others. There isn't any kind of creative streak at all, and that I find profoundly depressing. At this stage, with the way we've organised politics in this country, and particularly in the south, there doesn't seem to be any fresh blood coming into it. The young people who are coming into it are by and large people whose fathers were TDs – it's in the DNA. There are no new people coming in with imagination and vision for a new and better Ireland; it's all more of the same, all of the time, and I find that very depressing.

It obviously depends on how people other than me organise these events. There may be some smaller events organised by voluntary groups – different groups who might come up with some interesting ideas. Obviously the major events will be organised at official level, and I would pessimistically think they will be quite dull and quite predictable. But I still live in hope that interesting things might come out of this, that there will be a concentration of the intellectual and creative ideas of the people who were involved in all these events originally, and that it might lead to cross-community connections; that people will sit down and discuss things together, and out of our very difficult past construct some positive way forward.

Do events outside the country make much of this irrelevant? What you're talking about here is globalisation, and I think the interesting thing about globalisation is that, ironically, it actually reinforces national separateness. In spite of all the efforts of the international bankers, politicians and everything, you've got the revival of national languages all over the place, people reacting in a kind of converse way to the globalisation process, becoming immensely interested in their own culture and their own traditions.

So I don't like globalisation, I don't like what's happening at European level, I don't like the EU or the IMF having such a stranglehold on the economic and political life of the south, but I think it has an opposite cultural effect. People will actually be prouder of their own cultural instincts and their own cultural traditions. So they're not going to go away, you know, despite the best efforts of the bureaucrats, whether they be in Frankfurt or Washington or Brussels.

Robert Ballagh

My hope would be that this period – a good few years of various commemorations – will encourage discussion, debate and appreciation on all sides of the rich cultural and political heritage we share on this island.

IAN PAISLEY JR

Ian Paisley Jr is the son of Ian Paisley, founder of the Democratic Unionist Party. He served as a DUP Junior Minister in Stormont and is presently a DUP MP at Westminster.

Background

Politics was part of the informal conversation in our house generally – various events that were topical, that were newsworthy. There was also the human side of it; how politics was affecting the lives of my parents and later my sister, when she was in politics, and subsequently me.

I think the hurly-burly of what was going on in Northern Ireland dramatically affected my life. I grew up in a situation where there were police guards at our house, where for a period of time I had to go to school in the back of a police car. So that obviously had an impact, especially when I was a very young child. When your father carries a weapon – a gun – and you see that as a child, it does provoke thoughts as to why. I suppose those things became normal. When you look back on it now, with Northern Ireland turning a page and a chapter, they were very abnormal times. I had a wonderful experience about two years ago when my daughter said to me, 'Dad, I'm doing something in school in my history class. What were the Troubles?' It was a word she'd never heard, because it was history she was talking about, it wasn't actuality. She was fifteen then and her words were quite inspiring. Things actually have changed, because when I was fifteen, I knew what the Troubles were. I knew the effect of them, because your life was informed by them everywhere you went. Thankfully that has changed now and changed quite dramatically.

You can't do this job [politics] unless you really want to do it. I certainly am not the person to be forced into doing things I don't want to do – I just come from that ilk. So I don't think you could do this unless you really wanted to do it and you couldn't do it with stamina or pace unless you wanted to do it. Because it's not an easy life. There are 101 other things I could do that'd be more rewarding in all sorts of ways, so you really have to want to do it. I do, and I enjoy it.

The Centenaries

Some people think that things like 1912 happen with a bang – 1912, we'll have the Covenant. No, it was the culmination of twenty years. It really started in the 1890s with Gladstone and Home Rule, and the uncertainty over what was happening with Ireland and Ireland's position.

There hasn't been the same build-up to the celebration as there was to the event at the time. There has been very little thought put into the commemoration. Now I'm very glad that people are talking about it, and I know the Orange Order want to do something. I would love for there to be the same sort of enthusiasm that went into the event itself. Whenever you look back on the Ulster Covenant, consider the people who influenced it – the tycoons of industry, influential religious figures on the Protestant and Evangelical and Episcopalian side. Not only captains of industry and people of religion, but major politicians, from prime ministers down – I mean really significant figures. Now I'm glad I'm starting to hear words from the Secretary of State and indeed the Prime Minister.

These commemorations, of course, have to be handled appropriately. People have to be given space to celebrate in their own way and not have others try to interpret them for us. I think the people have an entitlement. My grandfather signed the Covenant in his own blood. I think I'm entitled to say what that means to me, not to be told by someone what it means to me, and I think that will be the feeling that will influence most people.

But it's good that people are now starting to put their mind to it, trying to shape it, and I hope we can do it in such a way that everyone learns a little bit more about each other. I mean, I've very little interest in celebrating the Easter Rising and the commemoration of it in 2016, but I'm enthusiastic to understand it, to understand why, and I'm certainly very interested in understanding the context of the Somme, which was going on almost simultaneously with the Rising. As to the 1912-2012 stuff, I certainly would be interested in making sure not only that I end up knowing more about it, but that the entire community understands why it was done, why it was so important. If you go back to the north of Ireland at the turn of the century, we had eighty embassies or consulates working in Belfast, because of our rope-making, our textiles, our shipbuilding. Today I think we've only two consulates. We were the dynamo of an industrial revolution, and I think that has been lost. We need to understand just how important Ulster was to Britain at that time, industrially.

In terms of the effect of the Covenant commemoration on the public generally, I would like them to realise that they had a cause, and to understand what that cause was about. It wasn't a narrow thing of just anti-Rome rule. It wasn't a narrow thing of religious wars, of Protestants versus Catholics. It was actually much broader than that. It was set in the industrial question, it was set as part of the empire question, it was set as part of the political question, it was set as part of the economic question and as part of the cultural question. I'd like people to understand that unionism is a much more complex ideology than some maybe give it credit for, who think it's some sort of sectarian ideology. It's not. It's much broader than that.

So I'd hope people will have deepened their sense of their own unionism through the centenary. And actually it's bang up-to-date – it will be quite important, especially if Alex Salmond is pressing more and more on the Scottish union question. The timing of this could be quite critical for the current union. If there is a wave of enthusiasm, a wave of understanding as to why the union was politically, culturally, economically and spiritually important to people, that might make for a reawakening of that body of thought across the whole of the kingdom, and that I think would be wonderful. It would be a real fillip to unionists here that we had helped save the Scottish union now, a hundred years later.

These things aren't taught properly in school. We should get back to the point where our kids are taught these things about their own history. We've got a rich tapestry of history. It's controversial, it pokes you in the eye, but that should not turn you away from it. If you study American history in America you learn about slavery, about civil rights – you learn about all sorts of things, and why, and whose side were you on. That question is provoked. I just hope that we can start to teach these things in such a way that people get to understand why people were so troubled as to sign a Covenant in their own blood, and why they were inspired to do it. This went right back to the Scottish Covenant in 1638, where it was driven from, and this became a Covenant between a man and his God as to what was important, and why he would disobey a nation. The Protestant tradition comes from the 1611 translation of the Bible, which put kingliness at the top of that pyramid, and yet they were saying in 1638 and then again in 1912 that they were going to reject that authority. That's pretty important – people need to grasp that.

As to understanding the Covenant a hundred years later, there can be different interpretations of it, if it is very well documented as to why this was being done. The problem is, people have gone for the easy argument: that this was about Protestants and Catholics. It was very largely no such thing. It was a bigger argument than that.

I think I can commemorate and cherish something that's about my culture, my identity, my history. I don't necessarily expect people who would be opposed to that, or have demonstrated an opposition to that, to understand it in the same way. But I've no opposition to people wanting to be a part of that and to understand it. After all, the Covenant did affect those on the other side of the argument. In the same way, I am quite happy to maybe not play a part in the 1916 celebrations if that's what they're going to be (which I hope they're not), but I would be happy to learn more about what motivated them and why people think about 1916 today. There's a lot of misinterpretation, as I say, about what 1916 was about.

There'll be Covenant events run by churches and events run by the Orange Order that will, I imagine, be for a specific audience. There should also be something done by our government, whether it's the government of Northern Ireland or more importantly the government of the UK. That would be a national thing and I wouldn't want it to be exclusive. It would have to be handled very carefully, but it should be delivered in such a way as to give recognition to something that happened in the past and to why it has shaped these islands.

If you were doing something nationally, I imagine that nationalists and republicans would be invited. Whether they would attend is something very different. I think most people still haven't got over the fact that they didn't attend Her Majesty's visit to the Republic of Ireland. But I wouldn't have a problem with people wanting to understand the commemoration and wanting to be part of it. At the same time, I wouldn't want it to be hijacked. We have a very sharp history, a very hard history, a very bloody history, and I'm the first to step back and recognise that a republican and a nationalist mightn't want to understand my interpretation of it [*Laughs*], or to think that they're there to be offended by me. We have to be careful in that. We should be using this to learn from history, not to repeat it.

In terms of commemoration deepening division: we're a divided people anyway. What is important is how it's handled and how it's managed. The fact that the union is so safe now – for a whole host of reasons, including the outcome of the political negotiations and the economic situation that we find ourselves in today – means that I don't think commemoration poses a threat. I think these things affirm, or possibly reaffirm, as opposed to deepen. I don't think the divisions of Northern Ireland get deeper every Twelfth of July; I think they might be reaffirmed. So I don't think it poses a problem. You could draw a blanket over the occasion but that's just crazy. The nations that forget their histories are destined to repeat them.

I think unionism sees the events of Easter 1916 through the eyes of the Somme, because it was very much a case of 'England's disadvantage,

Ireland's advantage', and there's the view that the Easter Rising was the stab in the back. I mean, Willie Redmond fought at Gallipoli or Ypres at the time the Rising took place, and lost his life. He was the son of a nationalist leader – that fact could be lost. And this is where I think there are some bounds. I've absolutely no problem with the Irish Government – the current Irish Government in the Republic of Ireland – taking ownership of the 1916 commemorations and celebrating, because it was from that event that part of Ireland seceded from the union. They've every right to explain and explore and develop their history. But there was hardly anything of a Rising in Ulster, and to try to portray something up here that didn't occur would be the airbrushing and rewriting of history. I think the focus has to be on what happened in Dublin. It was essentially a Dublin Rising – it was called the Dublin Rising in the papers at the time. I've absolutely no doubt that some people will want to usurp the occasion and use it as a political tool; we have to caution against that and say that would be silly. That's why I think the government in the south should take command and drive it. If they don't, they will be the biggest losers. But I'm much more relaxed about it now, given what's happened in the euro crisis and the eurozone, and all of the very meaty comments we have now in papers like *The Irish Times* and the *Irish Independent*: where is Irish sovereignty now, in the current climate? It's an opportunity for people to really explore that.

I'm an avid student of history, so I've absolutely no difficulty in exploring the Easter Rising further. As I say, the more we study, the more we learn from it, and hopefully we learn not to repeat it. Regarding attendance, I don't see why I would be inspired to attend. I've read about that history. It'd almost be like going and celebrating and understanding what happened in some of the death camps. I've always wanted to avoid going to Auschwitz. I'm just saying there are parts of history I'll learn about, read about, understand. There are dark parts of history that wouldn't inspire me to want to go and see it, or to want to go and commemorate it, but I would still want to understand it. Then there are other parts of history which I would be motivated to. I mean, I would be moved, and I have been moved, when I go to the Somme. But not the Easter Rising commemorations. It's just a feeling I have as a unionist. Why would I? And that's why I say, it's very great and glad-handy to say, 'I'd love to see republicans or nationalists coming.' I can put myself in their shoes – why would they want to understand?

I can understand why we should understand each other. That doesn't mean we want to be part of that commemoration. I would leave it to the individual, if an individual or even unionist leaders wanted to go. I'm just saying, if you're asking me – no. That's not to say that if I learned there was going to be something pretty incredible to understand … I mean, Bertie Ahern really rolled out the Orange carpet with what they did at the Boyne site. But that was a shared history of what happened hundreds of years ago on this island and it affected the entire island. There was an opening up and an understanding there, where we could cross the divide, see and understand it. Does that mean you're going to be rolled back as a nationalist? Probably not. But I'd canter back to the Boyne site any time [*Laughs*].

It's true all of the centenaries coming up are shared. But you put shared against sympathy towards it. I've a shared history in terms of what happened on this island. Am I sympathetic to what happened at the Easter Rising? No. Am I sympathetic to what happened in 1912? Yes, because I'm a unionist. Am I sympathetic to what happened in the 1920s? Yes. And I actually think that 2020 – whatever happens around that celebration or recognition – is probably going to be the most telling one. Because that was about cutting the island and saying that's how the succession will be handled, that's how it will be cut. I suppose these are two dry runs – 1912 and 1916 – for how we handle the big one in 2020.

I don't think you can do the centenaries all in one. They will all have to be given their own space – they happened at different times, in their own settings. If you're going to understand that, you have to see history through the eyes of its own time, not through the eyes of our time. And through the eyes of your political opponents. I think you should always try to put yourself in the other person's shoes. But it's broader than that. Everyone has something to learn. I've read about and tried to learn about risings in India and risings in Africa, because I've been interested in that colonial-type history and what happened. So I want to stress I've absolutely no difficulty with that. But do I want to then go and celebrate it? That's where I would run out of enthusiasm! [*Laughs*]

As to the Somme centenary, something will have to happen at the location of the Somme. In the current way, where you have all this positive feedback for our current troops, we have a really positive opportunity to try to set the Somme in terms of what it meant for the humanity of Northern Ireland – what Northern Ireland lost to it, in terms of generations, from the big house. Take this constituency [North Antrim]: what the McNaughtons lost with their two sons, and what a gardener got in that vicinity for his George Cross or his Victoria Cross in terms of bringing the bodies back. There are some really massive stories in all of that, things that make *Downton Abbey* look like a fairytale. Getting those things together and letting people understand that the blood of the people here wrote the history of the empire and wrote the history of this nation – that can't be forgotten about.

The Somme is where we really have lost something of our history, in that there were a lot more nationalists who went to war from the southern counties than has ever been given credit. Only now is there starting to be an awakening to that. As I mentioned earlier, there's Willie Redmond's story – the nationalist leader's own sons, one of them dying on the battlefield. Those stories need to be embraced and understood more fully, because that shows that we really did have a shared imperial history and imperial war history. I would have absolutely no difficulty with a joint commemoration of the Somme. I think it would be very helpful for southern Ireland to turn a page – a page that was blotted out – in the context of what Her Majesty did in the Republic of Ireland recently, in recognition of our shared history. It's going to be an awful lot easier for unionists, let's say, if they want to attend something like 1916. They certainly wouldn't be getting any brickbats from me, even if personally I wouldn't have much of an interest. I'm not ruling it out – I want to set it in that context. It will depend very much on the way it's shaped and what it's for. It could be something that is unmissable.

And who knows – there is a view that for 1912, something could be done jointly by governments, something could be done jointly in 1916, which takes it out of the hands of party politics and puts it in the sense of the national mood at the time and what they're trying to say. There might be something that could be developed along those roads and I'm open to that, if it's done right.

History, you know, is so complex: why one person would sign a covenant in blood and one wouldn't; why two people would sign it in blood but have very different feelings about it. Joseph Barber, the great linen-mill owner in Lisburn – he signed it for his economic future. I've no doubt he had religious and political and other views, but he signed it as a tycoon.

There's similar complexity in nationalism and republicanism. I studied what happened with Pearse. I think he was a lunatic. There were other people, however, who fought at the Easter Rising who had what I can only describe as noble ideals. They wanted to break, in the same way that people wanted to break in the previous century from imperial rule in America, from British rule. They had that ideal. I've seen the same thing all over the African continent, where people awoke and said, 'No, we want to move away from this imperialism.' I can understand that. But I can also say that Pearse was, in my view, a madman. In his own writings he compares his blood sacrifice to that of Christ's. Those are the words of a lunatic. I mean, he was going there deliberately to die. You go into battle to *win* – even if you know you're going to die [*Laughs*].

I don't think the centenaries will advance anything in terms of where we are politically or where we are as nations. What they will do is hopefully increase people's learning and people's understanding. Will it change anyone's views? There might be a few people around the fringes who'll say, 'Ah, I get it now!' Will it make republicans become unionists or unionists become more republican? I doubt it.

Look, the best thing about Northern Ireland, and indeed the best thing about Ireland, is it's so small and we all know each other, don't we? The worst thing about Ireland, and Northern Ireland, is it's so small, and we get on each other's nerves [*Laughs*]. I don't think there is anything out there that would convince anyone who is currently opposed to my views or my ideology, that would really convince him to embrace them. I think they might understand it more, but that might make them despise it more, in the sense that they really are wrong! In the same way, people who may study nationalism or republicanism or the Rising might think, 'Hmm – that was crazy!'

I hope the centenaries deepen people's sense of identity. I think there also has to be equality brought to how it's done. It can't be left to amateurs on one part of the island to do one thing and to governments to do something else on another part of the island – I think that's important. If the national government of the Republic of Ireland decides to drive this in their part of the island, then I think our government – Westminster – has a responsibility to be seen to drive it. Can an Executive that's made up in the way ours is drive it? I don't think it can, because of the complexities and differences that exist. But I think that our senior politicians and our national government have a responsibility, if the southern government does it. Remember, the Queen's visit was so positive because governments, at the most senior level, drove it. At the same time, unionists should take a hold of it – they'd be mad not to.

Because of what we've had, will the centenaries lead to a fresh version of the Troubles? No. I heard all this before Her Majesty's visit, 'Oh, this could spark things off. It's not the right time.' It happened, it passed and I think it's been an acclaimed success. While I don't know if these centenary commemorations will be on the same par, who knows? But they have the potential to be really positive, and they have the potential to be positive marketing tools as well. Why not seize the opportunity?

RODDY DOYLE

Roddy Doyle is a novelist, dramatist and screenwriter. His novels include The Commitments, Paddy Clarke Ha Ha Ha, *and* A Star Called Henry *(set during Easter 1916).*

Background

My family was Fianna Fáil – very much so. The Proclamation of Independence was in the hall. My father framed it and put some sort of a resin cover on it around about Easter 1966. His father was – in a casual sense – a founding member of Fianna Fáil, was involved in the War of Independence, was in the IRA, went the de Valera route, although he wasn't, as far as I know, involved in the Civil War.

But my father's first political memories would have been from the 1932 General Election, where he helped his dad put up posters. Sean MacEntee was the candidate, and my father remembers the big celebrations because Fianna Fáil won and he remembers the torchlight celebrations. I suppose it's saying a lot about Irish politics at the time and since: a big memory he has is grinding glass. Glass bottles were put into sacks, then hammered and ground down, then mixed into the poster paste. This was to stop the Blueshirts, as they were known (and are still known in my parents' house), and members of the guards from pulling down the posters. And he claims – although most of his stories should be examined – that sometime after he got married, in the early 1950s, he cycled out to Tallaght after work to say hello to his mother. It started raining and he took shelter under a railway bridge, and he found one of the posters that him and his dad had put up in 1932 [*Laughs*] – still intact. Worn but still there. So yes, it was a very political household. My father was an active member of Fianna Fáil for years and years.

Politics talk was constant. TDs would be in the house; my father was director of elections for Michael Woods, who was a member of the Cabinet for a couple of decades. I remember an election in 1982, I think it would have been, where I was canvassing for Noel Browne, a socialist TD in the neighbouring constituency, while still living in the family home, and my father was director of elections for Fianna Fáil in his own constituency. But it didn't lead to any clash, not really. I think by that point we both accepted that we were going separate routes. I tired of it very quickly, but we both enjoyed the whole political process, I think, and I still find it interesting. He grew up with it and to an extent so did I. In the household there were a lot of backroom meetings; the house didn't have a back room, but nevertheless there were backroom meetings.

My mother's background was not dissimilar. Her father, a journalist, was involved in the republican movement. As far as she knows he never had a gun, but again it was very Fianna Fáil – from a republican family in Wexford.

When I go to vote these days I vote Labour. I'm not a member of a political party and I couldn't see myself ever joining a political party. As a teenager, I suppose you want to be a bit different, a little bit rebellious. At the same time, I was aware that things weren't quite right, and I became increasingly aware, the older I got and the more I wandered around, that things weren't quite right, that there was a lot of unfairness.

I hated secondary school. I hated the whole school system. I went to a Christian Brothers' School and it struck me as being, in my final year in secondary school, just close to unbearable. I just thought it was wrong – fundamentally wrong. So I leaned to the left, I suppose. In retrospect, that was, in part, to annoy my father, which I can say quite cheerfully now because he's eighty-eight and we're fast friends. But there was an honesty to it as well. There was a new political party in my first year in UCD called the Socialist Labour Party – a breakaway from the Labour Party – and Noel Browne would have been its big iconic figure. I joined that and was very actively involved for about four years, but began to dislike the way that, for many people of the left, the people who were the enemy were other people on the left and not the real enemy. It was amusing for a while – a bit like *The Life of Brian*, with The People's Front of Judea and the Judean People's Front – but I think maybe after seeing *The Life of Brian* I decided I'd hang up my boots [*Laughs*].

The Centenaries

I think the centenaries overall will be looked at positively. Certainly people I know, south of the border here, have been quite open to the idea that there are more layers to being Irish than they were led to believe, and that's one of the reasons the Republic of Ireland is a very different place from what it was twenty years ago. There are people of my age, some older, some younger, just got tired of that very strict definition of what it was to be Irish, which excluded probably as many people as it included. The notion that we're 'Catholic Republican with a capital R' people – I don't believe people think that any more. Well, the vast majority of people don't think that any more, if they ever did actively think it in the first place. So the idea that being Irish could also mean being British is quite interesting. And I suppose we increasingly see the evidence right before our eyes – to be Irish and Nigerian, to be Irish and Polish, to be Irish and American, to be Irish and Irish – so I think there'd be a fascination with it.

There is a hole in our knowledge about the Irish involvement in the First World War, and I think that it in an intellectual way and – I hope I'm not being insensitive here – in an entertaining way it is a story that people are dying to hear. If you look at the Somme, for example, we all know the names of the big battles, but we were led to believe that, by and large, they were other people's battles and not our battles. Even though there was a statistic available about the number of people who died, there was very little known about it.

I haven't given the Somme centenary a great deal of thought, but a joint north–south commemoration would probably be a very good idea. I think the way the Queen's visit here in May was nuanced was quite brilliant. Using some of the brainpower that went into that visit to choreograph commemorations, celebrations, memorials, whatever you want, would be very, very good, I think. I was surprised by how moved I was at the Queen's visit, particularly when she went, on the first day, straight to the Garden of Remembrance – that was just extraordinary in its simplicity. I knew it was going to happen and I thought it was a good idea; it was a long time coming. I remember taking a bit of time off work to watch her arriving at the airport, etc., then I went back up to work and came back down at lunchtime and watched this, and I was – yeah – I was close to tears. I might even have cried. Then, the next day, it seemed perfectly right that she should go with the President and pay the equivalent tribute to men who had died in the wars.

There's a bit of family in it as well, because of my father's father and his uncles – one of them went off to join the army and fought in Salonica. As legend has it, he went off a hero and came back something of a traitor. Then he joined the Free State Army and he fought against his brothers, one of whom died in the Civil War. That's a huge canyon to run through any family – a typical family in South County Dublin.

I don't think commemoration of the Covenant and of Easter 1916 need be divisive, although it could be. I mean, if you look at the Queen's visit again, because it's still fresh; that was an opportunity for people who wanted to throw stones to throw them, and a couple of dozen did – some of whom were wearing Manchester United away jerseys! [*Laughs*] So I suppose the Ulster Covenant events will be an opportunity for people to express themselves in that way. I don't know about the south and the Covenant. It would be good to read about it and try to find out a little bit more about it – to see the humanity behind that huge granite depiction of Carson and maybe try to figure out the thinking behind the signing of it.

As for Easter 1916, I honestly don't know. I believe the Shinners already have booked the Mansion House – they were way ahead of everybody else [*Laughs*]. There's no escaping the fact that it's a great story, the 1916 Rising. Actually they're all great stories but it's a fantastic story, a terribly romantic story. I think – I'm not saying this with any great confidence, in hope as much as anything – you might have ructions, but I get the feeling that after that the rubble will be cleaned up life will go on as usual.

Commemoration already has started a debate. It's a fascinating thing in a fictional sense; I have tried to write about it, especially in *A Star Called Henry,* particularly in the last volume. When I sit back and look at what's been going on for the last twenty-five years, thirty years – well actually all my life – it's not so much about the geographical control of the country as control of the definition of the country, the definition of what it is to be Irish. I think the bit of wealth we had for the last twenty years was a great loosener; old definitions became a bit less relevant. It may well be that, because times are harder and they're not getting any easier, there'll be an electoral opportunity between now and 1916, that there could be the emergence of an extreme force. It's unlikely but it's not impossible.

I would hope not. I suppose some of us would have been waiting with bated breath in the last election for somebody to come out and say, 'There are X amount of foreigners in the country, there are X amount of Irish people unemployed; if we get rid of the X amount we'll have employment.' Nobody said that out loud and you kind of breathed a sigh of relief. I'm not sure if it'd get much of an ear anyway, but nobody said it, and I think if anybody thought it would have a sympathetic audience there would have been plenty of people queuing up to say it. Because of this notion of who controls the definition of Ireland, I think there will be a very loud, terrific, and in some ways a healthy debate about 1916.

There's no doubt about it, the signing of the Covenant and Easter 1916 are two diametrically opposed events. But again, it's all down to who we are. At the moment, to a degree, we're kind of lost. For a while we were, as it says in *The Commitments*, 'the niggers of Europe'. More recently, then, we were the great success story of Europe, and we got that kicked out from underneath us. That confidence we had, particularly south of the border, in declaring ourselves European, that's been badly rattled now as well. So it literally is the case that we're a bit lost. And that could be a good thing.

But who are we and what is it that we want? I think it's interesting in Ireland at the moment. There are those saying, 'Why haven't we protested as they've done in Greece? Why haven't there been riots? Why haven't there been huge protests?' And there are those who would like them. I personally find our own approach to what's gone wrong far more interesting; in some ways it's reassuring, in other ways it's worrying. It seems to me that we've taken it on the chin, but at the same time we're waiting with bated breath for things to get back to normal again.

Nineteen-sixteen, in the minds of a lot of republican people, is 'Year Zero'. Then the Provos took as their holy grail that direct route from 1916 to 1921, and the Army Council were the government of Ireland. It's not now. The big issue is, what is Ireland? Where are we? Are we on the edge of Europe, are we at the centre of Europe? I think there's a good opportunity for that kind of healthy debate in the next few years – because nothing's going to happen very quickly – using 1916 and using 1912, and the Somme. I think the time really is ripe. The President of Ireland wearing a poppy is a hugely symbolic thing, and it happened. Laying down wreaths at the memorials to those who would have been branded traitors – it's happened.

For the first years of our marriage we lived in a house in Killester that was built for veterans of the First World War. The whole little estate was built – there are several of them around Dublin. The men who lived in those houses used to meet at what is now the Artane roundabout and march into town in November. And they had to do it quite ...secretly, I suppose. But it's a bit like other stones that have been lifted and examined in the Republic of Ireland, where there have been apologies and some attempts to include people who were very deliberately excluded from society. I think in a less extreme way that's a stone that has been, is being, and will be lifted. There were thousands and thousands of men who went off and were written out of the official version of history. When I was a kid, in secondary school, in primary school, there was a very linear way of giving us our history: a direct link from Cuchulain and the Fianna, up through St Patrick to the men of 1916. That was the history we were given. When the bombs started being planted in pubs, that version of history, I believe, disappeared, and actually there was no real teaching of Irish history in Irish schools for quite a while. Both extremes are unhealthy, and I think some form of debate – although it can obviously be a bit unpredictable and therefore frightening – would be a great opportunity to talk about what we are.

I believe the centenaries are richer in potential than just having separate commemorations. This is the way we do things; let's get on and do it. So for example if a group of people here decided they wanted to commemorate the Ulster Covenant next year, grand. I mightn't go; I might watch it on telly. If there are documentaries, and I'm sure there will be, I'll watch some of them. I'll pick the best and watch them. I'll be interested in it – I won't feel hostility towards it. Easter 1916? I honestly don't know. I remember when I was eight, for the fiftieth anniversary, there was a wonderful television drama, four nights in a row – written by Hugh Leonard, I discovered later. It was great. I was an eight-year-old watching it and it was brilliant in many ways. Then there was a debate; I remember sitting down on the fifth night to watch more and there was a debate on instead. My parents watched that but I was devastated really. Instead of a programme about men fighting there was middle-aged men talking! [*Laughs*] It was a bitter disappointment. I don't know if there's anything in the planning, but there's nothing like a really well-made television series to get you thinking and reacting, so that could be good for the Ulster Covenant as well.

A bad commemoration of Easter 1916 would be if it was unquestioning. I don't think it'll happen. In school, the men of 1916 – and the few women – weren't human, ever. They were saints. And for Irish we did the short stories of Pádraig Pearse, and some of his poetry. I mean, he's not one of the major prose writers of European literature. It was awful sentimental trash. But the Christian Brother and the lay teachers who taught us Irish, presented this stuff as if it was Biblical, you know? Unquestioning.

There should be questions so that we give back these men their humanity. Let's see human beings making these decisions, flawed and all as they are. Let's see the vanity of them, for example, the bad decisions that turned out well, and the seemingly clever decisions that turned out terribly. The British officer who decided it would be a good idea to execute the leaders – I'd love to see a proper depiction of him. And not as a beefy public schoolboy who has come in to teach Paddy a lesson but as a human being, to understand just what sort of pressure he was under. A good, well-told story would probably be brilliant. And 1912, for that matter. Wouldn't it be great to have a good, well-acted series, with some great Irish character actors as working-class men queuing up to sign the Covenant? That'd be fantastic. It would do more than any symposium. People would watch it and be moved by it. And while they mightn't come away sympathetic to the cause, they'd certainly come away sympathetic to the people who lined up behind the cause, so to speak. Television probably has a huge role to play in the next couple of years.

Personally, I am looking forward to the 1916 thing but I don't know if I'd see it as cause for celebration as such at the moment. If I was invited by Sinn Féin to come to something in the Mansion House on the day I'd be saying no, because I don't have much in common with Sinn Féin – although there's a lot to admire in how they've redefined themselves in recent years. A lot of brave thinking went into that but I still don't like a lot of it, you know [*Laughs*]. And I'm not sure I'd go to any government celebration. I'm not sure about celebrating but I'm interested in it at the same time, so I could be quite pernickety. I could end up reading nothing but stuff about 1916 in the year 2016 and at the same time say, 'No, I didn't celebrate it.' But somehow in my head I am.

I think there was a link between the fiftieth anniversary of 1916 and the decades that followed – and the coincidence of the IRA blowing up Nelson's Pillar. But I think most people in Dublin disapproved of that and quite liked the pillar, and felt the absence of that for a long, long time in what is one of the biggest streets in Europe. The public has been thinking about a thirty-two-county republic anyway. It's literally the case now that you'd wonder where the border is or was. It's still there. It's a bit like the Berlin Wall. I was there before the wall came down and I was there a couple of years after the wall came down, and it was easy to see where the wall had been.

I think the 1916 Centenary is unlikely to change thinking about a thirty-two-county republic, but, if well choreographed, it could soften attitudes. A very well-made TV drama series, for example, could allow loyalist working people to feel closer in feeling to nationalist working people of that time and place. If some of the brainpower that went into choreographing the Queen's recent visit goes into the centenary, it could have a positive impact – assuming a thirty-two-county republic is a positive. However, there won't be one centenary celebration – there'll be ones by the State, Sinn Féin, Fianna Fáil, Fine Gael, even Labour, etc. We'll more than likely have a Celebrity Chef 1916 Special!

I've a feeling that the combination of centenaries could bring people closer together. People in the Republic are now happy to accept the First World War as part of their history. I know several friends who recently went to Belgium and France to visit the sites where their grandfathers fought. One only found out about his grandfather's wartime experience recently. I don't think the centenaries will sharpen divisions. Again – I seem to have become suddenly very fond of the word 'choreographed' – it depends on how it is done. If the stories of the young men – and women – who were at the centre of these events are brought to the front, they could have a colossal impact.

NUALA O'LOAN

Nuala O'Loan was the first Police Ombudsman in Northern Ireland, from 1999 to 2007. In 2009, she was appointed to the House of Lords and became Baroness O'Loan of Kirkinriola. In 2010, she was appointed chairman of the Governing Authority of the National University of Ireland, Maynooth.

Background

I was born in Hertfordshire, grew up in Yorkshire. My father died when I was thirteen, and no, politics wasn't there at all – survival was the issue for us [*Laughs*]. The first time I became aware of Northern Ireland politics was Bloody Sunday; I remember going to the House of Commons and queuing up to get in, the Monday after. I was studying in London.

I came here five years after that event, but it was my first introduction to the fact that there were major problems in Northern Ireland – problems beyond the scope of anything I had imagined could exist within the UK. So when Declan wanted to come back and live here after we'd graduated and qualified, I thought about it, because I knew there were Troubles here. But I had no idea what Troubles actually meant, and I decided that was all right, we'd be safe.

My first introduction to the politics of Northern Ireland, I remember, was sharing an office with some people who kept asking me which school I went to. I kept telling them I went to a girls' school, a boarding school – I'd various answers for them. So I said to Declan, 'They just keep coming back and asking me which school.' He said, 'Just tell them it was a convent and that'll solve the problem.' And it did! Then I began to realise that it was important; it had never mattered before, which school I went to.

Then Declan became involved in politics and I watched. I never joined a political party; I could not possibly adhere to the strictures of one political party. But I watched.

The Centenaries

The first two centenaries – the Signing of the Covenant and Easter 1916 – definitely have the capacity to divide people. The third one – the Somme in 1916 – maybe because I grew up in England, I would see as different. To me, the tragedy of the First World War is surely greater than our Catholic–Protestant issues. But it cannot be celebration, that I do know. How any commemoration of it is handled will be immeasurably important, because the marching season commences on 17 March, and the potential for generating something in a society which is now economically seriously disadvantaged, with all the consequential problems of unemployment, might be serious.

My understanding of the 1912 Covenant is that it could be construed as being anti-Catholic, and therefore it is celebrating that which is trying to denigrate a part of the community. I think in a way that's why the Twelfth marches can never be celebrated by Catholics; it's what lies behind – and not just what lies behind, but what the people who are celebrating think they're celebrating, which may be a different thing from what they're actually celebrating.

I think a conference very carefully crafted, which brought together different interpretations of the 1912 Covenant, would be a very good way to manage its commemoration. What it was about? What lay behind it? Who were the characters? Who were the players?

Marches? No, I don't think so. A Jesuit called Alan McGuckian is working on a project on commemorations. They have created a drama and it is intended to engage people with their prejudice, with their understanding, etc. I think the key thing for me in all our history is that we can understand and know what did happen, rather than the myths around what happened.

Memories are very long in Northern Ireland but I think some things do change. I think the understanding even of what happened in 1916 ... I mean, recently I've heard almost a revisionist approach to Easter 1916 which suggests that it wasn't quite the way that it's presented, as a glorious fight against the British. So I think things do change.

But a deepened prejudice would be my concern about celebrating the 1912 Covenant. At the same time, there is something around growing understanding and coming closer together. I think it could be done but it'd have to be done in small workshops and things like that – I don't think grand occasions will enable that sort of enhanced understanding. Commemorations are opportunities – opportunities to enable people to come closer together.

I think you could start off by looking back to where Ireland was before 1912. The reality was that Ireland, north and south, was abandoned by the British – during the Famine, for example – to a very significant extent. There was huge poverty here. We had our landlords; maybe not to the same degree in the north-east, but in the north-west and in other parts there were very significant problems.

If you start then from the perspective of the tradition that has its closest links with England, and always looks that way and never looks down south, and actually had no wish to be engaged with the southern people; it was all right when they were part of the British Isles, but to become part of the island of Ireland seems to have become something that was anathema to them. I think if you could begin to understand why they felt like that, and yet simultaneously understand that the carving out of this very prosperous part of the island of Ireland, keeping it separate for a group of people almost, was bound to lead to what happened at the end of the day. You could argue that 1912 is responsible for everything that followed. I wouldn't put the blame on the unionist people for what has followed; I'm just saying that that act of separation which followed the Ulster Covenant was the key to everything.

But I'd be optimistic that reflection might be productive. I would hope so. I know that a lot of people are thinking about it and I know a lot of effort is going into trying to ensure that it is both inclusive and reflective. I attended a British–Irish conference this year and that was the subject. It's the subject of a lot of meetings I've been to, so yes, I do think that attempts are being made to ensure that across Northern Ireland it is not something which causes further division.

As for 1916: it was a point in time, wasn't it? It wasn't the end of the story, as such. Just as the 1912 Covenant was a point in time. But 1916 has a much greater image. People understand the Proclamation and all that sort of thing, so there's a greater familiarity with it among southerners. If we just look at the nonsense that goes on up the hill at Stormont over whether you can put lilies out at Easter – that alone tells you something about how things are viewed. My understanding is that, at Easter, there is a resistance to putting lilies in the hall – the Great Hall at Stormont – in celebration of, or in recognition of 1916. Lilies are symbolic of Easter, but they are also associated with 1916, I think. So that has presented itself as a problem over a number of years. I think they may have resolved it now but I'm not altogether sure they have.

I think it's different for the south and the north, because from 1916 came the creation of what became the Free State – the Republic of Ireland. There was a setting-free of the people of Ireland from colonial rule, which could only be a good thing. So I can understand why they would want to celebrate. In the north, 1916 in a way consolidated the fears that the unionists had; and the separation then of the six counties was almost inevitable. I can see that for them it would be different and difficult. But I think that since it's in the context of a national identity, it's right that it should be celebrated. And I think it's right that we should respect both, and therefore perhaps have a more reflective, a more inclusive, more creative celebration or commemoration.

I had a view of 1916 which was informed by the books I'd read to date. But I've seen more and more recently that questions whether 1916 had to happen at all, questions what actually did happen. So I'd like to learn more about it and maybe there are others who'd like to learn more about it. I think it's bound to have a different meaning in the north, because the north is not part of the Republic of Ireland. That has been the stated aim of the nationalist parties and therefore, in a way, commemoration gives them a reason to renew that desire and that aim. The fact that Articles 2 and 3 of the Irish constitution were changed doesn't address the issue for the northern nationalist population. It's inevitable that they will want to claim that and to claim the right to nationalist identity – in reality, rather than just something that they're claiming. So I think that that will be or could be very problematic. Of course the current Irish economic situation may have an impact on that, but I think there'll be celebrations as distinct from commemorations.

People have the right to celebrate – freedom of thought is profoundly important – but it could be counter-productive. There will be commemorations of 1916, undoubtedly; there'll be a bit of political huffing and puffing around symbols and things like that – and then we'll get on with life. I don't think it's likely to lead to conflict or to effect a change in public attitude. The people of Northern Ireland, where the potential for conflict is probably stronger, have experienced so much conflict and have suffered so much that they have decided they do not want that any more. That's why the dissidents, although they're there, have not managed to gather over the years. They were bombing right through 1998, but Omagh was thirteen years ago now, and yet the dissidents seem to me to be at the same or a lesser stage of capability and capacity. So no, I don't think it'll lead to further violence. It could lead to further division if it's not properly handled. It would be more creative and more enriching if, rather than deepening a sense of nationalism and unionism, you were able to deepen a sense of the other's understanding of history, to a point where you were able to accept the other in a better way, to move forward as a society. I think that would be the best outcome.

I'd welcome the presence of republicans at a commemoration of the signing of the Covenant, but I don't think it's likely to happen. Depending on who was developing this particular event, they wouldn't get an invitation in many cases. They might get an invitation from the loyalist paramilitary and they might accept that invitation. At that level, you're most likely to see points of interaction, curiously enough. But it would only be republicans who would have had associations with the IRA and not the dissidents.

Equally, I'd welcome the presence of unionists at commemorations of 1916. They may well get an invitation and I think some of them would accept it. I can think of individuals who definitely would accept it. But there are others who, if they were running this celebration, would see it as triumphalist, and then there would be those from the other community who, if they were invited, would see themselves as compromised by attending. But there is a richness in the peoples and there will always be those who will go. There would be those at the more official level who would make this step, but I would think that, equally, there would be those who would have another engagement somewhere.

I suppose at the moment, I've heard so much about what the likely outcome might be – in terms of enhanced division, in terms of enhanced sectarianism, physical damage to property, rioting; and then moving across the spectrum, something that enables people to embrace each other a little more – that I just don't know. I don't know what the outcome will be and I don't have a sufficient grasp of what might happen to be able to be either positive or negative. But that doesn't mean I'm neutral; it means I'm questioning. It has the potential for good, our history, if we can understand it better. I mean, Auschwitz has the potential for good insofar as, if we can understand what happened, we realise it must never happen again. So that which is so profoundly evil still has potential for good. Likewise in the commemoration of these two events, which are the product of history, I do not see them as being incapable of producing good – on both sides of the community.

The commemoration of the Somme is likely to be less contentious, because the soldiers who died at the Somme came from right across the community. They were representative. Huge numbers of Catholics died at the Somme and huge numbers of Ulstermen died, but others died too. My grandfather was in the army. He joined from Dublin in the early 1900s, probably for economic reasons. He survived the First World War but was badly wounded. So maybe I come from a slightly coloured understanding of why the Somme should not be divisive. I also have a nephew who lost a leg at the age of eighteen fighting in Iraq, having walked out of school to help the Iraqi people be free, and suffered terrible injuries. I have another nephew who's currently in the army and will go to Afghanistan again. So maybe my colours are sort of prejudiced there. But to me the Somme is the absolute, ultimate obscenity. All those young men fed over the wires into the machine guns, knowing what was going to happen to them, living in those trenches in the dirt and the water and the rats … No, I feel very strongly that war is such an obscenity.

I think the Somme centenary should be done with dignity, with sadness, with determination … because people now are talking about another war. I mean they're talking about the economic situation having the potential to lead to another war. It wouldn't be a war, in the same terms as 1914-18, but it would have the same capacity to destroy lives and countries. And I think, therefore, if we use the Battle of the Somme in any way, it should be to remember the atrocity. I suppose I'm of the Wilfred Owen way of thinking – '*Dulce et decorum est*' – the old lie. No, we should remember it in those terms; we should remember those poor young men. It's such a tragedy to think of a generation wiped out like that.

For some people, because of the connotations of the British Army in Northern Ireland, they will disengage from it, they will not want to be engaged. But I will be very surprised if there's any attempt to disrupt it or anything like that. In the south, I think there's a recognition of the reality that a lot of people went from there to fight in the First World War – and there were other places besides the Somme, let's face it – and therefore they have something to commemorate too. We saw that recently in the commemoration by Mary McAleese and Queen Elizabeth.

I think these centenaries are an opportunity for learning. There are a lot of people trying to ensure that this time is used positively and creatively. There will be inevitable incursions into boggy ground, but we have so much to battle at the moment, in terms of our economic recession and the social difficulties we have, that our energies should be concentrated on the positive rather than anything else. I would hope that would be where we will be.

MARY LOU MCDONALD

Mary Lou McDonald was an MEP (2004-2009) and is TD for Dublin Central. She is Vice-President of Sinn Féin.

Background

I suppose by tradition my family would have been anti-Treaty – Irregulars, Fianna Fáilers. But that was just a happenstance, I suppose, of the classic Civil War politics. And yes, we talked about politics, and not just domestic politics. My mother in particular would have had a keen eye to places like Burma and the international scene, and she would have been a member of Amnesty International. So that would have been the stuff of debate and conversation in the house.

In terms of republican politics and the national question, I remember thirty years ago when there was the Hunger Strike in the blocks, I remember the no-wash protest – I remember all of that imagery being beamed into our home. I remember my mother's reaction to it, the broader family's reaction to it, the frustration, the anger. I remember as a child not fully grasping what was going on or why, but understanding something deeply traumatic was happening. There wouldn't have been any difference of opinion between us on that one, but there would have been on others. And in the broader family circle there would be difference. I would typify my family as traditionally Fianna Fáil but there's a couple of Blueshirts lurking in there as well. I don't think that's untypical, so I suppose I come from a pretty typical southern nationalist background.

My interest in the world around me and in politics was informed by my family and home atmosphere. For me it was a very conscious choice to become active in party politics. When I was at university, I was actively interested in different campaigns but I wasn't a member of any political party. Then time moved on, I started in the real world, and I came to a realisation that, if you really want to change things and you're serious, you have to engage with the party political system. I was in Fianna Fáil for a while. That was, if not the easy place to go, the most accessible. I had friends in that party – I still do. But it was obvious very quickly that I was in the wrong place. Then, some time later, I came to know republicans, Sinn Féin members and so on, from different campaigns. I was a member of the Irish National Congress along with Robert Ballagh and Finian McGrath, who is now also a TD. And that's how I came to join Sinn Féin. It was a conscious decision on my part, because there wouldn't have been a whole pile of people that I knocked around with, that I had been to school with, that I worked with, who were signed-up members of Sinn Féin – it was kind of unusual.

I had been up and down to the likes of Portadown, the Ormeau Road, in the days when the marching season was really difficult and the peace process was just taking shape. I'd been up and down to Belfast, been to a number of public meetings. But I think the time that I said, 'Right, this is it', was when I went to hear Adams speak in the Mansion House. The place was thronged and I remember there was a very heavy Special Branch presence outside. I went in with a friend of mine and she was laughing and saying, 'Well, great!' [*Laughs*] She wouldn't ordinarily, let's say, have been going to Sinn Féin meetings. But Gerry spoke that night. I remember there were one or two in the audience who were quite aggressive with him – they were kind of ceasefire soldiers, as they call them. I admired the way he handled himself. I said to myself, 'These guys actually know what they're doing.' I saw in the Adams leadership and in the politics of Sinn Féin potential for the fourth green field and the thirty-two-county Ireland to be more than just rhetoric or a ballad sung at a bar counter late in the night. I think in that moment I decided, 'Right. I'm going to be part of it.' Not with the intention of running for elections – I didn't have a big elaborate plan or anything – but I just thought, 'This is serious, this isn't messing. This is serious politics with a huge opportunity to change things.' And whatever wee bit I could do I figured I would do.

The Centenaries

I wasn't born at the time of the fiftieth anniversary of the Easter Rising, but I've heard tales from people, so I have a sense that it was a seminal moment. I think inevitably when anniversaries or centenaries come around, people revisit, and either challenge their own analysis or confirm their own analysis. But I think it's a bit off-the-wall, quite frankly, to say that the conflict that ensued north of the border was caused because we marked the fiftieth anniversary of the Easter Rising. The reason why there was conflict up north is because you had an oppressive one-party state that actively and brazenly discriminated against a particular class of person. That's what happened. And because the island had been sundered and partitioned. Although I wasn't there at the time, I imagine the fiftieth anniversary sharpened the perception and the realisation and the challenge for the political classes, but that it was the cause of the conflict is very wide of the mark.

The commemorations of the Covenant and Easter 1916 could deepen the fissure between people, but I don't think they will. Let me tell you why. I believe that the Ulster Covenant is a moment for unionism and loyalism to take stock. A lot will hinge on the nature of leadership and the kind of broad narrative that's established by lead players as that commemoration happens. What will be the content of that? There will probably be those who will try to use it as a rallying call and for a sort of negative dynamic, but there'll be a lot of others who will analyse it in a different way – from a historical perspective, but also in contemporary terms. Yes, it'll be about reaffirming identity, because unionists are unionists, they believe in the union and they're entitled to that point of view. But because it comes in a cycle of other centenaries and because of where we are now politically, I don't think that you could talk about or understand that event in isolation. And so I believe there'll be a more sophisticated linkage between these events. For unionism the marking of the centenary is a moment for reaffirming identity, but also for trying to place that identity in contemporary terms, because you're a hundred years on. Maybe it's time to have a discussion: 'What value is the Union now?' – in circumstances where the Orange state is gone; single-party rule has been consigned to the dustbin of history; you have the power-sharing institutions, the All-Ireland institutions, Section 75 and the equality provisions. We live in a global village now and we're in huge economic crisis now – Ireland north and south. We'll either hang together or we'll surely hang separately. So the dynamic now is very complex and very interesting; what value the Union now? If there was to be a Covenant signed by the loyalist and unionist people of our country next year, what would it be? What stand are they taking and is it still the traditional? I think there's a big discussion to be had there, and of course you'll have your hard-liners, you'll have your traditionalists. In life we can stereotype each other, but just as republicans aren't robots or sheep or made to order out of a catalogue, neither are unionists or loyalists. People are complicated and people are smart, and people live in the here and now as well as having their baggage.

I would hope there'll be nationalists and/or republicans attending commemorative events for the signing of the Covenant. And I would go further than that: I would hope that we might consider, as republicans, marking that centenary. Because as different and as fraught as the relationship has been, and still can be, between loyalism and republicanism, unionism and nationalism, we're part of each other's story too. So the loyalist narrative only makes sense when placed beside the republican turn of events and experience. We don't make sense if we isolate each other: we're part of each other's story, as well as having our own separate narratives. We're just out of our Sinn Féin Ard Fheis, where the leadership of our movement was saying, 'The Republic is for Catholic, Protestant and Dissenter. We have to reach out to unionism and understand unionism.' That can't just be rhetoric, that has to be real. So if invited, I can see no reason why I wouldn't attend a commemoration of the signing of the Ulster Covenant.

Regarding Easter 1916, I imagine there might be unionists in the south as well as in the north – or partitionists, maybe [*Laughs*] – who would look at this and say, 'This could become a jingoistic jamboree,' or they might see it as something along those lines. We need to be conscious of that. Do you remember when we rediscovered the commemoration of 1916? It was under Bertie Ahern's government. I can't remember which year, but they had a big brouhaha outside the GPO, and there were planes flying and soldiers marching – it was very smart, and I respect that kind of military stuff, I don't have a hang-up about it. But we need to be careful that the centenary celebrations don't become about that. Ireland is not a military superpower, thank God, with all the hardware and paraphernalia of war, and I don't think we should ape that. And yet the insurrection was of the physical force variety. It was violent and it was a physical force confrontation, involving weapons. But the Rising wasn't about that. The Rising was about the men and women of Ireland, the children of Ireland, about political concepts, about good governance, about the sense of the collective, the marshalling of common resources, the distribution of wealth – things that really matter. And the centenary commemorations, to do justice to the Proclamation and the women and men of 1916, have to reflect all of that. It can't be about a couple of planes flying over O'Connell Street, some kind of exclusively militaristic glance at things. There's space for everybody.

The Dublin Government will do its thing and certainly we'll be planning political events. I presume other parties will do likewise. But I hope it won't descend into anything crass or ludicrous. The important thing is that we get back to basics and honour the Proclamation. It always strikes me that at Easter time, particularly at the state commemoration, someone from Óglaigh na hÉireann steps forward and recites the Proclamation. All the political establishment are there in a very sombre and solemn mood, and you just think, 'If you people had any sense of irony whatsoever, you'd hear in that Proclamation the most damning indictment of the state [*Laughs*], line by line.' I think the trick would be to find ways of commemorating that which would do justice to everything, so that it's a historical celebration of people in a particular time and place, but the ideas of the politics of it have to triumph.

Particularly given the circumstances we're now in. I mean, economic sovereignty is now lost and the IMF are in running the show, so there's a real resonance now that there wouldn't have been five or ten years ago, particularly in the southern state, around the concepts that underpin Easter 1916. We have to translate that into celebrations and commemorations that people can participate in, and that are open for everybody, whatever their politics, to take an interest in, and a part in. I know there had been an Oireachtas committee established to determine the state-run events. It had been meeting and then it stopped meeting, so we'd need to follow that up when I go back to the Dáil.

Regarding the Somme, I think it would be true to say that for a very long while in nationalist Ireland, it maybe wouldn't have been the done thing to brag or to put an over emphasis on the fact that members of the family had fought in the British Army – irrespective of where they were or why they were there. I do think that has changed. There's probably a bigger comfort level now, in terms of publicly discussing it. That said, I think in some quarters the pendulum has swung to nearly the other extreme. Certainly with some media commentators, when they talk about the Somme, you would imagine that there had been billboards across the Free State prohibiting any discussion or reference to these matters or to the soldiers that fought and died. So there's a need for a wee bit of balance. It's a period of history that is now being revisited more frequently because we've made political progress, and there's more scope for it.

It's interrelated, too, with the peace process and the political journey we're on now in modern times – it opened up the space for it. It's also used not simply as a celebration of those men who fought at the Somme and elsewhere, but as a competing point for the public consciousness to rally around. I dislike when this happens but you can see it sometimes in the public discourse – that the Rising didn't happen really, that it was almost a local wee skirmish; the real heroism and the real action was at the Somme. I absolutely detest when that happens – trying to draw those kinds of really invidious tensions between totally different events. You probably know the writers who do it: Battle of the Somme – brave, romantic, naïve Willie McBride; 1916 or anything associated with Fenianism – grubby and dangerous and criminal. There's still that tension there and for a couple of commentators that's their view, their analysis of it.

I think the time is ripe for initiatives like a joint commemoration of the Somme. There is no reason why that couldn't happen. That can happen and you still can have the unionists going home to their unionist homestead, the republicans going home to the Falls Road, the Markets or wherever, with their ideology intact, their view intact, their identity intact. I hate the clichés around this, but it is genuinely about understanding the other and being challenged by it, but not getting knocked off kilter simply because somebody has a different story from you.

There are those who'd argue for completely separate commemorations: the Proclamation and the Somme for unionist, Easter 1916 for republicans. The people who might make that argument, say from the unionist community, could then make the commemoration a rallying point for reasserting their Britishness. That's fine. You could take the view on the other side of the fence that we celebrate the Rising and so on to reaffirm our Irishness. Fine. But if you simply do it that way, you miss all the potential in the middle, because there's a lot to be learned about the Battle of the Somme. Some of it is around respectfully remembering young lives lost and very brave people. But there's also a story there about global wars, about the working classes as fodder for imperial wars. There is a republican analysis of the Battle of the Somme and of the First World War, as it's called. I don't think anybody should be force-fed that, or that it should be used to insult anyone, but I think anyone who takes an interest in that war must at least consider why Willie McBride was there in the first place and Willie McBride's experience while he was there. Because it wasn't the war to end all wars – it happened again and again and again.

The same thing goes for the Rising. If we as republicans commemorate not just the sequence of events in Dublin in that period of time, but really commemorate the Rising, it would be nearly perverse to do so in a way that would exclude anybody, because it's about inclusivity.

In the first instance, we as republicans need to listen. I am genuinely very interested to hear what will be said. What will come from some quarters is predictable. But I'm really hopeful. When the Revd Latimer came and gave a very rousing contribution [*Laughs*] to the Ard Fheis, he said some things and used terms which surprised me. It was really interesting – he had nearly co-opted our vocabulary. So I hope there will be interesting things said and I hope that we as republicans will have some interesting things to say about the Covenant, bar the standard established assessment of that period of time and how unionism was rallied.

If you and I were around in 1912, we wouldn't have been signing the Covenant [*Laughs*] – I think it's safe to say that. But it happened, it's a historical event and you have to have an analysis of it – draw some learning and content from it. And I think that in all of our cultural DNA and all of our history, things happened that shouldn't have happened. But they happened and they've now become part of our tribe's story. So that's what the Ulster Covenant was. And for me, unionists can say, 'That's as it was then, that's how it is now' – Sin é – and kind of ignore the world around them, or they can say, 'That happened, we're still unionists, but what is the union about now?'

If centenary commemorations are just about a brass band and waving flags, okay, we'll organise that in two weeks. If it's to be anything worth writing a book about or worth really talking about, it has to happen at some other level; not just for the academics and the very learned, but for Joe Public – for regular people like us. Unionists have to say, 'Why the union?' In the same way, republicans have to say, 'Why a united Ireland?' And I think now we realise – all of us within the republican family – it's not just enough to say 'A united Ireland' as a slogan. We actually have to convince people that this is the rational, democratic way to go, and how you would go – the nuts and bolts of it.

How do these ideas relate to Europe and globalisation? Anyone who sees national sovereignty as old hat has to be challenged, because if the southern state's woes prove anything, they prove that it really does matter that democratically elected and accountable governments make decisions on raising taxes, spending taxes, and funding and organising the social services that that really matter. I was in the European Parliament, and I see the huge value of that kind of model in many ways, but it is incredibly dangerous to strip political control and sovereignty and vest it in a super-national structure in a concentrated way, because those on the periphery and those who would be deemed to be weaker in economic terms have to go along with that. It's time to either put up or shut up. With the euro entry there wasn't even a debate around it. Just, 'We won't have to change our money on holidays, yippee!' No discussion of the downside of tying yourself so tightly to a monetary policy that would be driven and designed to suit the massive German and French economies. And here we are now. So I don't accept that it doesn't matter. To my mind democracy is best organised at its most local level. The further down you can drill it into the grassroots, the better.

But I'm optimistic. I'm very optimistic, and I think you would have to be a pretty negative person, in the Ireland of 2012 or 2016, to view those centenaries as negative. There will of course be those who will use those centenaries to bang a particular drum, while the vast majority of people, depending on the event and the community, will mark the event with a level of pride and remembrance. But if we're worth our salt at all in this country – I don't care what your view is on the constitution – it's a moment of reflection as well. Where are we? What are we at? What's this all about? For republicans and nationalists, it's around the united Ireland issue. Where is that now, and how does our generation conceive of that? How do we convince our unionist brothers and sisters as to what their place in that might be? Because I have a view that sometimes unionism and loyalism completely misunderstand what republicanism is about. I know that's a result of us having such a prolonged and deep conflict, but unionism has to make the case for the union. They can't go, 'Oh, but we've got more than 50 per cent so feck off, that's how it is!' What's the case for the union? That's the challenge for them.

GREGORY CAMPBELL

*Gregory Campbell is a leading figure in the Democratic
Unionist Party. He is an MP at Westminster and an MLA
at the Stormont Assembly, where he has held a number of
posts, including Minister for Culture, Arts and Leisure.*

Background

I came from a family that was political in the sense that they would have voted all the time, but there was no participation, no membership, no active political consideration. It was the Troubles that nudged me into politics, being born where I was born, when I was born, with the violence erupting. I was sixteen when the Troubles started, so it was just being plunged into that which brought me into politics. I've heard colleagues of mine say there was a specific event that brought them into politics; with me it was just a combination of things. It was frustration, annoyance, disturbances, parades, protests, and then shootings. A combination of things.

I was brought up in Londonderry, born and raised in a small terraced house about 300 metres from the first civil rights march in Duke Street. I know there was one before that in Tyrone, but the famous 5 October 1968 march – I was born almost on the route of that. And I got involved. It was more from a sense of anger and frustration at a nationalist agenda that was being vigorously pursued and the ineptitude of unionism to respond to that. I just wanted to get involved in helping, as a teenager might. So if there was a meeting I would put out leaflets for it, if there were posters to go up about a counter-demonstration or something, I would do that – anything that a young person would have put their hand to in trying to promote a small 'p' political agenda. But at that stage I never envisaged getting involved personally.

In 1968-9 particularly, there was this view that I had, that I know was shared by many thousands of my co-religionists, that there was a nationalist agenda. That nationalists were complaining about not having jobs, but we didn't have jobs. Nationalists were complaining about not having civil rights, but we didn't have civil rights; nationalists were complaining about standards of living which we didn't have. And there was no point in a simplistic analysis of, 'Why didn't you join the civil rights movement?' because for a unionist that was anathema. Why would we want to join something that wanted to destroy, in our view, the country that we loved and we share? The media were swallowing this story hook, line and sinker, and there was no unionist to stand up and say, 'Hang on a minute, do you know what the reality is here?' There was just that extreme frustration that bit at me like a cancer, which said, 'You've got to do something. It doesn't matter that you're only fifteen, it doesn't matter that you can only hand out twenty leaflets – do something!' It was either that or join what was the fledgling UDA, and I didn't want to go down the violence route.

Gregory Campbell

The Centenaries

There's a working party on events like the 1912 centenary. I don't know what the outcome of their deliberations will be but I know there'll be a series of events to mark the centenaries. There is an issue – and I think it's not just in unionism, it's in nationalism and it's prevalent across society – that younger generations don't attach the same degree of significance to historical events that earlier generations do. Now that might be the passage of time: as we all get older we think that, just as policemen look younger now, younger people do actually attach a significance that we don't see expressed in them. But I would like the younger generation to see the significance of those events and to act in a way that shows they appreciate the relevance of those events, even if they were 100 years ago. Whether that will pan out in terms of the actual events, we'll have to wait and see. But that's what I would like. And I would like to see it deepen their sense of unionism. If we look at the Covenant, there are many people, young unionists today, who would just take Northern Ireland as a fact, as a status quo, as no big deal to get worked up about. They have no deep abiding sense of how and why Northern Ireland came about. And the Covenant is, if you like, the anchor from which the ship that became Northern Ireland eventually set sail. I think that sense of awareness exists among my generation and maybe even down to those in their forties, but I suspect that in the eighteen to thirty-five age group there isn't as much awareness. And if the commemorations deepen that, that'll be a good thing.

Likewise I would presume republicans would want their commemoration of 1916 to deepen their sense of republicanism. Although looking across the divide, there is a sense among unionists that there is already a deeper sense of awareness in the republican community about their sense of history than there is in unionism. I see a fairly deep awareness in the republican community. Whether that's reality or perception on my part, I don't know.

I don't think that the commemorations should deepen division. What these events are designed to do and what they should achieve is a sense of awareness of the historical roots of our society. But there should not be an automatic correlation between that and 2012; commemoration does not mean regressing in terms of where we are in 2012, that we in some way awaken a sense of division rather than a sense of, 'That's where we came from and that's part of my belonging.' In the same way, I suppose, that any other divided society might look back historically. I mean there'd be no sense of re-imposition of apartheid in South Africa if the Boers were to commemorate some famous event in the past that some people in the black community might take exception to. And that's not to equate the two positions, between Northern Ireland and South Africa. It's the same in America, it's the same all over. A commemoration of an event 100 years ago should not mean that divisions which are still pretty real today are reawakened or deepened, rather than the event simply being a commemoration of where we came from.

There are two ways of looking at republican commemoration of Easter 1916. If you have a simple republican community's commemoration of the Easter Rising, then I think most unionists will say, 'Well, that's part of their history.' It's a bit like 15 August, the Ancient Order of Hibernians' day. Someone might say, 'I don't particularly like it, I don't share it, I don't engage in it – but it's their day, let them get on with commemorating it.' If the celebration or commemoration of the Easter Rising is done in that context, I don't think there'll be a problem. Where there may well be a problem is if some element in the republican community wants to say, 'Not only do we want to commemorate the Easter Rising, but we want to do it in a way that brings 1916 over to 2016, in the sense that the guns, the violence and the murder that was enacted on the streets of Dublin in 1916 are going in some way to be replicated or exonerated or magnified in 2016.' Unionists might say then, 'Well hang on a minute, does this mean that there's going to be some sort of glorification of murder re-enacted on the streets of Belfast?' I think you'd be into a problem then.

I don't know what the Easter Rising people have designed for commemorative events, but let's say they had some kind of re-enactment of the shooting of British soldiers on the streets of Dublin in the Easter Rising and did it in a way that glorifies the death of the Brits ... the Union Jack steeped in blood or something. I can just envisage ways in which people could do it; a re-enactment of what happened but done in such a way as to make the community who believe and are passionately a part of that British identity feel very, not just uncomfortable, but that they haven't gone away, you know. In other words, this is a re-enactment of the old system, the old way of doing things, and somebody here is saying to us as unionists, 'Well it might only be a pageant, but we're just letting you know that if things don't go right, we can go back to what we do best.'

I'm reluctant to get into what unionists might see as a good form of commemoration for Easter 1916, for the very simple reason that if I am going to talk about something, whether it's a commemorative event or any type of event that unionism cherishes, I'm very loath to take advice about how I should do that. Now if I take that position, would I then be more than a little hypocritical to say to republicans, 'Well look, we don't mind you celebrating the Easter Rising, but we don't like the way that you do it. Could you do it another way please?' Then they're going to say to me, 'But you won't take any advice about how you should celebrate the Ulster Covenant.' I think there has to be a degree of sensitivity within each community about how they celebrate their own commemorative events, being mindful that if they give advice across the divide, they have to be prepared to take it. If they're prepared to say across the divide, 'Well actually we don't want any advice,' then be prepared for the *quid pro quo*.

In all honesty, I can't see as many pitfalls or possible areas of contention with the commemoration of the signing of the Covenant. If you've some sort of re-enactment of the Covenant, the actual deed of signing the Covenant, and the historical context, I don't see as much potential there, except were you to have some sort of re-enactment of gun-running or that, that then that might be perceived by nationalists as being, 'Well, if we don't get our way, we'll go back to what we do.' But the actual commemoration of the signing of the Covenant shouldn't hold the same potential for problems for nationalists that I can see the Easter Rising might for unionists.

The Battle of the Somme commemoration has the least potential for division, because you had not only the 36th Ulster but you'd the 16th Irish division, and I think maybe twenty or thirty years ago, when there wasn't the same degree of understanding in the nationalist community of what the Somme meant to unionists, there might have been the possibility of nationalists not understanding. But I do think that due to the work a number of groups have done this past ten or fifteen years to widen the understanding – I would be amazed and extremely disappointed if there was division on the commemoration of the Somme.

With the Covenant signing, you need to examine how the position got to where hundreds of thousands of people, some in their own blood, signed the Ulster Solemn League and Covenant. If you do that and you examine the historical context of that time, you then see that the Ulster people – unionist people in Ulster at that stage – saw that there was a definitive time in their history coming about when, if the British Government were to proceed along a route they had tried to proceed previously, in terms of the Home Rule Bill, in Kipling's words, we were gone, we were finished, it was over. So it was a defining moment in that it became almost the midwife to the birth of Northern Ireland. It's a bit like the Siege. I always say, while unionists in Northern Ireland celebrate the Battle of the Boyne, had the Siege of Derry not been won, there probably wouldn't have been a Battle of the Boyne and we wouldn't have had what we commemorate today. The Covenant is a bit like that. The unionist community all celebrate the birth of Northern Ireland, but had there not been a Solemn League and Covenant, there probably wouldn't have been a Northern Ireland to celebrate.

I use the 'context' word a lot because I think it is important. Local newspapers, when they tend to look back a lot, often show snapshots of twenty or thirty years ago, and they're quite popular because people are constantly looking back. I'm getting to the stage in life now when I see events of twenty or thirty years ago, and I see things that I said twenty or thirty years ago, I think, 'Why did I say that?' And the only way you can understand it is you've got to get a grip on what was going on at the time. Was there a protest? Was there a march? Was there a statement? Was there a speech? If you simply look at that in isolation, you say, 'What on earth was that about? Why would somebody have said that?', until you go back and look at what led up to that.

So you have to look at the Covenant in that light, in that context. And the context was that the unionist people of Northern Ireland had, for 120 years before that, been citizens of the UK – Britain and Ireland. And the government of their country was choosing to say to them, 'I'm sorry, at a given point in the short term, you're no longer going to be part of the kingdom of the nation that you belonged to for so long. Because of a variety of other events, we're actually proceeding down the route of the Home Rule Bill,' which in unionist perception meant, 'That will mean the end of the UK as we know it.' So they attempted to overthrow that in parliament: they went through the democratic route and it didn't work. So the context was, 'We've tried all democratic means, now we've got to show the government that we're not prepared to give up our citizenship.' That was the context in which that happened. I don't expect nationalists will say, 'Well that's fine, that makes everything wonderful,' but that's the context.

I suppose the Somme has a resonance today, because some people would look at the conflict both in Iraq and Afghanistan and praise the bravery of the soldiers involved there, while at the same time as questioning the wisdom of sending them in the first place. I suppose you could translate that and go back 100 years to the Somme. But that is always the case. In every battle, generals and political leaders will take the decision, and be that decision right or wrong, there are then the ground troops, the tens of thousands that have to go into battle on foot of whatever decision has been taken. There is a sense that the First World War, as opposed to the Second World War, was just mired in a series of ill-judged decisions by a series of generals and politicians, but I don't think that the unionist community will be as much interested in whether that was a worthless or not worthless task. The whole relevant point was that almost a generation was prepared to put itself on the line – young men from across Northern Ireland. There was hardly a street that remained unaffected. I think of the famous words of the English colonel – I forget his name now – who was there at the Somme. He said, 'I'm not an Ulsterman but on 1 July 1916, as I dwelt with the 36th Ulster Division, I would give anything to be an Ulsterman, because of the heroism and the bravery I saw as the men went over the top.' That sort of loyalty and tribute is what's going to be remembered, rather than the decision that put them there in the first place.

My belief in the value of the union is not economic at all. The proof that it's not economic is very current, because whether the Republic was going through the Celtic Tiger boom times or going through the bankruptcy times they're now going through, the unionist position is the same. So if anybody is looking for proof that it's not economic, it's in the past twenty years that you see the proof of that. Because the Republic was a veritable goldmine twenty years ago and we said, 'We still don't want to be part of you.' It's not even the link. It's the innate sense of Britishness. It'd be the same if I went to the streets of Glasgow. If we set aside the ardent Scottish nationalists or the Alex Salmond types – I know they're a sizeable bunch – the average Scots person would probably be more proud of his Scottishness than he would be of his Britishness, but he still would say, 'But it doesn't diminish my Britishness. It's not a case of am I Scottish or am I British. I'm both.' And I'm the same; I'm an Ulsterman and I'm British. It's a sense of belonging, of being. It's nothing to do with the economy. Obviously we'd prefer a better economy than in the Republic, but whether the Free State is blossoming or bankrupt, it doesn't make any difference to me. I'm still British. And an Ulsterman. But not an Irishman.

I think unionists need to be saying to nationalists, 'This is an intrinsic part of who and what we are; whether it's the Somme or the Covenant, it's an essential part of our being, of our politics, of our history, of our background. It's just who and what we are.' But there's no sense that any of those commemorative events should be viewed in a combative role or a confrontational role. Within the confines of what I said at the very start of the interview, I don't think they will be seen like that, as long as they are presented in a suitable and appropriate manner, which I think they will be. I don't see why nationalists should view them in any other light. I don't expect nationalists to warmly embrace them but I expect nationalists to say, 'It's the unionists' day, let them get on with it.' Just as I would expect unionists to say of nationalists in terms of the Easter Rising, providing it is done in the way I said and it isn't in your face ... 'This is what we'll go back to if we don't get our way.' As long as that isn't done, I would expect unionists to say likewise.

As to nationalist or republican attendance at commemoration for the Ulster Covenant or the Battle of the Somme, that would be a matter for the nationalist and republican community. I would imagine if they did, they would say, 'Then I presume some unionists will turn up at the Easter Rising event.' It would be a natural follow-on from that. And I certainly wouldn't be comfortable going to Easter Rising events. I would see the Easter Rising as a nationalist event but it's an event that celebrates the murder, the mass murder, of people like me. So I just find it a bit odd [*Laughs*] to celebrate how my antecedents were murdered. I just find that a bit odd, that people should think it a good thing that I would celebrate that. I think a more reasonable approach would be if I say, 'If they want to celebrate that, it doesn't bring me any great joy, but let them celebrate, provided they do it in a way as I've outlined.' It's just that I don't see the celebration of the Somme or the Covenant as being a celebration of the murder of nationalists – that wasn't what that was about at all. I wouldn't in any way say that nationalists and republicans shouldn't come to Covenant or Somme events. If they want to come they should be made welcome. By all means. And similarly, if unionists want to go to the Easter Rising events, they should be made welcome. If they want. I just don't know why unionists would want to do that.

The problem I have with the viewpoint that these events are divisive is that the corollary of it is, if you don't have those events, you will actually move away from the deepening of the division of the past. I just don't accept that. Some people believe if you go down this commemorative route you will reawaken old divisions, pick at the scab that's starting to heal. Therefore, don't do it and we will heal better and more quickly. That's to try and say that these events are in some way the source of division. I don't think they are. They are part of what we are, whether it's the Easter Rising or the Covenant or the Somme. I don't accept the premise that says, 'Hold them and you cause division, don't hold them and you will heal more quickly.' Because the divisions that are supposedly there – and we've seen evidence of them over the last thirty-five years – are going to be there whether these commemorative events are held or not. A Rangers–Celtic match can make divisions worse, the Twelfth of July can make divisions worse, but does anyone think if you cancel a Celtic or Rangers match, that Protestants and Catholics will come to the peace line and say, 'Well, the past is over'? I don't just accept that.

In the recent past, we had issues of schoolchildren on their route to school in North Belfast. I'm not getting into the pluses and minuses of all that, but it didn't take a re-enactment of the Battle of the Boyne to cause that. It didn't take a Rangers–Celtic match to cause that. That was an intrinsic part of the divided community that it took a whole cocktail of events to bring about, which is what we have. Anything on any given day can reawaken that. I just don't think that commemorative events fall into the category 'This will divide and cause division'. Particularly if people are mindful and cognisant of the way in which they have the celebrations, they shouldn't go down that route but will be seen as, 'This is what we are, this is how we are, how we came about.' It's nothing to do with creating a division in 2012 which didn't exist twenty or thirty or a hundred years ago. So I hope to be an active participant in two of the three centenaries [*Laughs*].

FR BRIAN D'ARCY

Brian D'Arcy is a Passionist priest based in Enniskillen. He is a newspaper columnist and broadcaster, and has written over ten books.

Background

Our family was nationalist but not republican. We were Catholics living in a townland that was completely Protestant and strongly unionist, but at the same time, my father's father was a member of the British Army and was killed in the Dardanelles on 15 August 1915. Although I never saw him, a picture of him in uniform was on the wall and he certainly wasn't denied; but nobody knew anything about him, including my father. It meant nothing at all to us. My mother's family were Corrigans, which would have been a republican family, and indeed her father was badly beaten on a number of occasions by the Black and Tans. So you had these two family things coming together. We were total Gaelic people but my mother would say, 'Don't get involved in the IRA.' There used to be Easter Sunday ceremonies in our local graveyard; some families would have stayed for those orations, the rest of us went home.

When I was a young boy we went on the bus to St Michael's in Enniskillen – about a six-mile journey – with neighbouring pupils from Royal Portora School, the Collegiate school. In fact, we walked together – St Michael's and the Collegiate were right beside each other – maybe two miles up the hill and we were very great, as young fellahs would be, with the girls that were walking with them up to school. The convent school was in a different direction altogether. You had all these farmers' sons of Protestants and Catholics who had far more in common than working-class sons like I was, of either view. Class did bring people together. The farming community was one and the working-class community was the other.

But there was another division – between those of a nationalist background and those from a unionist background – because, you see, the B-men were the problem. Among the boys going to school it was never spoken about. The way we got over it was that the ones going to St Michael's spoke Irish on the bus [*Laughs*] so that nobody else could understand. I mean there was no malice in any of it at all. But in school – we were taught by a priest – there was a kind of nationalism taught that was almost like Judaism, in the sense that it was linked to religion. Politics and religion became close. And then, of course, for two months of the year the two communities were utterly separated. None of us could get up and down the road, as they marched up and down, preparing to go to the Twelfth of July. And then 12 August was also a big day, so there was no peace until 12 August. And then on 15 August we had our sports and every Catholic went to that event. So it was insidious. No one ever told me but there was a pattern of life that was based around these things.

Politics has definitely played a huge part in my priestly life, no doubt about it. I've had to think and work hard at it because I came from that segregated background. I spent a little time in South Africa, because our order is working in South Africa, in Botswana, where there is that whole idea of segregation and division. In South Africa it was particularly difficult because you had the Afrikaaner Churches justifying apartheid from the Bible – an awful way of looking at it. Some people, like Bishop Hurley in Durban, were great heroes to me. He was a white man, originally from Offaly, long before Archbishop Tutu, a man who was walking with his black people long before there was any of this. And so all of these things came together in my mind.

I met de Valera as a student – he came to Mount Argus as President and I was asked to accompany him around and I had a conversation with him. Where I grew up, around Enniskillen, you could be arrested – many men *were* arrested – for shouting, 'Up Dev!' And here I was, standing beside Dev! [*Laughs*] Sadly he was quite blind at that time but he was an absolute gentleman. In fact he had taught mathematics for a Passionist school before he went to the Holy Ghosts, and he had in his mind that little connection. So Dev, to me, was also a hero and in many senses still is.

I happened to be ordained in 1969, exactly when the Troubles began, so from my first day that was what was going on. I went into journalism. Tim Pat Coogan and Fintan Faulkner in *The Irish Press* said, 'You have connections up in Ardoyne. Would you go up and please interview the chief of staff of the IRA for us quietly? We're not going to publish it but we might publish what you write on it.' And I did that, not knowing what I was going into. I was brought to him in Belfast, to his house, with a coat over my head in the back of a car. I had no idea where I went. I interviewed him and wrote up a report, so that Tim Pat and *The Irish Press* could have a better understanding of the IRA. My whole theme of this was to try to grow out of being prisoners of the past. When my mother died, before I was ordained, I suddenly discovered that the

Protestant neighbours were wonderful. They thought very highly of my mother and they were the first in with buns and baked bread, and that meant more to me than anything. That stuck in my head: my perception of these people was wrong.

My mother kept children of Protestant neighbours while they went to celebrate the Twelfth of July; my father milked the cows for a Protestant neighbour, George Lee, while he went to the Twelfth of July. In return George Lee would loan my father the tractor so that we could cut our meadow around that time, because we wouldn't have had a tractor ourselves. And so the bartering and the friendliness and the decency of people rose above the dictates of politics. That is what my theme has been all up the years.

The Centenaries

I remember the fiftieth anniversary of the Easter Rising very clearly. I was a student in Dublin, going to UCD, and the debates about the value of republicanism in UCD were tremendous. Many people who became leaders in politics afterwards, like Gerry Collins and people like that, were part of that group. They had amazing debates, which were eye-openers for me. Going to school, Pádraig Pearse and the 1916 men were absolute heroes – untarnished heroes – and Edward Carson of the Ulster Covenant and the Ulster Volunteers, and the William Craigs, were the baddies. As a student I went down on the bicycle to see the parades passing in O'Connell Street, and of course there was *Mise Éire*, with its wonderful music. There was a documentary arising from that, produced by Telefís Éireann, which was magnificent.

I've no doubt that people thought differently after the fiftieth anniversary, and so did I. Very quickly it seemed that it wasn't as black and white as I thought. In part, that was because of people like Fergal O'Connor, a quite magnificent lecturer in politics in UCD. I took his course even though I wasn't doing it as part of my degree. He was a great man for challenging your ideas about things, that this was a blood sacrifice – 'I see his blood upon the rose'. Besides this, Pearse and a number of others were closely associated with Mount Argus. Pearse brought his men to the Good Friday service there in 1916. He brought many of them to confessions, knowing that they were going to be killed in the 1916 Rising.

I would have had Fianna Fáil politics from home: *The Irish Press* came into our home all the time, and that's what it was. Then all of a sudden this was challenged for me. The only ones that ever challenged me before that were unionists, but now these very good and responsible and solid citizens from the Republic challenged me, with the kind of republic they had established and the kind of constitution that they had brought in in 1937, with a special position for the Catholic Church. Many people would have argued that de Valera was wrong not to listen to Archbishop John Charles McQuaid, that he should have made the Catholic religion the established religion of the Republic – which to me is an absolute contradiction in terms. How can a republic have an established religion? De Valera, in fairness to him, stood against that and got in this special phrase as a sop to John Charles. There was also the Mother and Child issue coming from that.

There was a perception that the men of 1916 were a crowd of crackpots with no support. There were sixty-four republicans killed. Nobody spoke about the 560 people they had killed in the Rising, for which they had no support at all. And did breaking the link with Britain solve anything? Did it serve the country well? Those were the questions that were being asked. What about de Valera's lack of support in fighting fascism? Because he didn't join with Winston Churchill in fighting the awfulness of the Germans ... Oftentimes what happens is, when minds broaden, then all cultures become examined. And that is a good thing. The problem is, when we are brainwashed, we're easily led. And that had happened to me, not only regarding republicanism but with Catholicism as well. In other words, by the fiftieth anniversary of the Rising, I was growing up.

I think that in general, the people of Ireland were grown-up after the fiftieth anniversary. From that point, elections became very difficult for one-party systems. Fianna Fáil tried to bring in single voting as distinct from proportional representation but that was defeated. People began to think for themselves. You no longer had it that the Church, Fianna Fáil and the GAA were the only sources of truth within the state. Other sources of truth came.

What effect will these three centenaries have? I don't know. We're in a very difficult position; the economy is so bad that doctrinaire politics has to take a back seat. If you read the Covenant, you'll see that God was definitely on their side. Similarly, if you read Rudyard Kipling's famous poem 'Ulster 1912', which is an eye-opener – so different from the pleasant 'If' poem. This poem shows a very bigoted power of God on the side of the Ulster people. And that led to the arms import and gun-running. Gun-running is now a republican sort of thing, but of course the biggest campaign of gun-running was that of Carson, and the police allowed it. When the same guns were brought in for the Irish Volunteers in Dublin, the police shot the people who brought them in. So there was different treatment all along the way. There's a sense in which the values of the 1912 Ulster Covenant and of the UVF subsequently gave permission for the equally doctrinaire and violent 1916 Rising.

The fiftieth anniversary of the Rising, certainly began a discussion that changed the face of things. What I would love to see – I don't know whether this will happen or not – is unionism, Protestantism, etc., examining its conscience. Is fear the best basis for political interaction? Or defence? And I'd ask for republicanism to do the exact same thing. Is our greatest enemy Britain? That'd be a great question for republicanism to answer honestly. Economically now we see that Britain isn't our biggest enemy.

About 1970, there was a wonderful old man called John Quinn, who owned H. Williams Supermarkets. He was born from the soil of Monaghan and he spoke as resolutely as Kavanagh did, and sometimes with the insights of Kavanagh. I was lucky enough to become a friend of his, because he used to come to half-past seven Mass – the only man I ever saw come to half-past seven Mass in a Rolls Royce! [*Laughs*] I spoke to him one morning and we became very good friends. I was editor of *The Cross* magazine at the time. He disagreed with almost everything I said but he admired the spunk with which I said it, and he allowed *The Cross* to be sold at the checkouts of H. Williams supermarkets, and to take its place, not as a religious magazine but as an organ of respectability. John used to philosophise greatly and he said, 'All these republicans talking about 1916 and victory. Now,' he said, 'go down O'Connell Street and who owns O'Connell Street? Every single major shop is a British-owned shop. They have conquered us by television and money, and they won the real war. We won the skirmish.' [*Laughs*]

My fear is that the Covenant commemoration will become a drum-thumping, Lambeg-banging, possibly even wooden rifles commemoration, which will be just the wrong memory. I think people have a right to commemorate what they thought was the defence of their religion and country. I'm sure they could say, 'A hundred years on, do we really need to behave in the same way?' We can become prisoners of the past. Was it Eoghan Harris that had a wonderful little example which I saw recently at a Liam Lynch commemoration? He has this great story of Liam Lynch and de Valera, anti-Treaty comrades, walking on an anti-Treaty rally one day. Lynch says to de Valera, 'I wonder what Tom Clarke would think of this?' And Dev answers, 'Tom Clarke is dead, our problems are our own.' Now that philosophy is a good philosophy. We shouldn't forget our past – republicanism and unionism. They're certainly valid, both. But we now have to ask, 'In the Ireland of today, in the world of today, in the Europe of today – can we be as segmented and can we be caught as prisoners of that tradition?'

Because what is unionism? Unionism with where? I mean, Britain has decided that they can't be on their own, they're not an imperial thing – they're part of the European Union. Likewise, Protestantism and Catholicism are both dead in the water as institutionalised Churches. Spirituality isn't dead, the expression of religion isn't dead, but because both of them held onto pasts that were unnecessary, I think the world has bypassed them. That applies to Protestantism in its many forms and to Catholicism in its many forms. We need a broader picture to come out of that and we need a republic that looks at the value of its citizens. The citizens aren't the same; there are now immigrants from all over the world. There are Polish people, there are Muslim people, there are Jewish people, and the majority has no religion at all. Now, what has republicanism to say to them? Where can unity come in? At this moment, if it weren't for the GAA in most of Ireland, there would be no sense of solidarity or community. It's the only thing left holding us together.

Easter 1916 was saying – and indeed it's echoed right to this day by all Sinn Féiners – that a united Ireland is the only answer. Now what do they mean by that? I can't get anybody to explain what it means. Where's the unity? I would like to challenge how the entrance of Martin McGuinness into the presidential race in the south was viewed. He was all right to be a ruler up there, but he's not good enough to be a ruler down here. Now where's the unity in that? The unionists probably would be right to say he belongs in the north, but the difficulty is that until quite recently, nationalists looked to Dublin for a solution and unionists looked to England for a solution. After many years of war, both of us have had our saviours wash their hands of us and say, 'Look, you have to find a solution for yourselves.' Now I'm not sure that the Good Friday Agreement is the perfect solution, but it's a hell of a lot better than what we had, and it has given us some sort of model to work on, though I'm not sure it can be a permanent one.

If you philosophise about your past, you should be able to say, 'It was of its time and they were strong men with a good movement.' I wouldn't denigrate those people. But can we expect people of a hundred years ago to offer a solution to our present world? Remember, there was no radio when those things happened, there was no television, no internet. There was very little travel, there was no unity across the world, there was no vision of a different world. Now how can you say that the solution of a hundred years ago is in any sense a solution for us today? We have to solve our own problems.

For the three centenaries to be commemorated productively, we'd have to see the futility of war as a solution to anything. In all three we'd have to recognise the futility of trying to force people into a way of acting. If there was one word that I would like to see brought out of it all it would be 'respect' – respect for culture, respect for difference. Respect for culture doesn't mean lack of unity. A republic that I believe in, a genuine republic, respects the individual's right to be different. It acknowledges the majority view but it also acknowledges the right to be different and the right to be yourself. I don't know what being a republican means if it doesn't mean that.

For example, it's an extraordinary thing that unionism rejects republicanism here and almost universally accepts republicanism in the United States of America. I can never figure out how that happened. Equally so, I can never figure out how all Irish Catholics support the Democrats over there and support republicanism here. Could we ask where our philosophies come from in all of this? Do we really have an understanding of monarchy, unionism and republicanism? There is a sense in which you could say that republicans rejected the monarchy of Britain and unionists rejected the monarchy of Rome. Maybe as working-class people we're saying the same thing; that we have some right to have our own legitimate philosophy accepted and catered for within our own island. It's maybe too much to hope, but I'm hoping there are enough thoughtful, educated people who can look at the fallacies of brainwashing that we have all endured, to our cost.

I think what would be very helpful would be, to begin with, an acknowledgement that mistakes were made on both sides. Could we have an apology for the futility of killing? Could we have that from the unionists? Could we have an apology for gerrymandering to such an extent that one voice was not as powerful as another? Don't forget, the Natal province took the Ulster Covenant as its basis for apartheid. Is that a wonderful thing to send across the world? Maybe equally we could have republicans doing a little more than Gusty Spence did. Gusty Spence, as far as he was able, began to make some apologies for the fallacies of his beliefs and the dangers that they had. But I think what Gusty Spence did is overestimated.

I also wonder if Sinn Féin is the only representation of republicanism left in Ireland, now Fianna Fáil are gone? Is there no other representation of republicanism than Sinn Féin? Where did the Protestant republicans go? Where did the Armours of Ballymoney go? Where did Roger Casement go? I mean, it was the Ulster Covenant really, and opposition to it, that brought Roger Casement to the fore. Unless I'm reading history incorrectly – which I could well be doing – that's where it came from. Now, where did that philosophy go? I'm not the first to say this. I honestly believe that if we looked at that type of opposition to popular thinking, we might discover that it isn't a completely black and white issue.

There are many citizens of Ireland – and I would consider myself one – who believe, 'I'm a Catholic, but I respect unionism and I respect Protestants.' And over the last twenty years that I've lived in the north of Ireland, I have discovered that there are many Protestants – wonderful, strong, good Protestants – who want to march on the Twelfth of July but don't see it as putting me down to do so. And I don't accept that they are trying to put me down. Similarly, I hope that they don't accept that I'm putting them down when I go to a Gaelic match and cheer my heart out for Fermanagh (and it doesn't happen too often!). Yesterday I helped to conduct a funeral in a Protestant church. Where I grew up in Bellanaleck, it was a mortal sin for me to enter a Protestant church – I would have had to go to the bishop for permission. So there is progress.

The commemoration of the Somme can be the most productive of the three centenaries. I would not have been a man for commemorating the Somme, but the more I've got to know about it, I've come to realise that so many Irish soldiers were part of the British Army in general. I had been brainwashed to believe that this was a British victory or a British Army thing, and that therefore I couldn't support the British Army in anything, even though my grandfather was in it! And I began to realise – my grandfather didn't want to fight for anyone. He had no other job. That was why he was prepared to do it. It's as simple as that. There were thousands upon thousands – possibly hundreds of thousands – of citizens in the south who went and fought, not because they wanted it but because it was the only job they had.

But do you know what it could come down to? Whether we wear the poppy or whether we don't. I think that would be a disaster. The Somme is the one that I'm most afraid of because it's more worldwide. The Ulster Covenant is Northern Irish, Easter 1916 is southern Irish. Then there is the huge thing of why Pádraig Pearse and these boys took advantage of the British Army, when they were fighting a world war against slavery in another place.

I'd be most afraid it could become a celebration of war. I think we should respect those who fought, but maybe they didn't fight for the same principles as those who had the time to think about why they were fighting. They fought because it was a job and had no other choice. The officer class were able to philosophise about war, but the working class fought it for them.

I don't know if I'll be attending any of the commemorations. I'd want to know what the philosophy behind it is. This is where a president can work much better than an elected government, as we saw in the invitation to the Queen, which had a very big effect on people, and dispelled some of the myths about royalty and majesty and monarchy and so forth. Mary McAleese did a tremendous job on that. And it wasn't just Mary McAleese, but also those who backed her – the Fianna Fáil Government, who did all the work for her before their collapse. So I think that if there are people like that around, who can think out a good way to take part in all three celebrations, in a sense of respect for unity, respect to disagree, I will then take part. But I'm not going for blood-sucking, thumping platitudes from the past. That's not what I want.

BERNADETTE McALISKEY

Bernadette McAliskey (née Devlin) was a leading figure in the People's Democracy party of the late 1960s. She was elected as a Unity candidate to Westminster in 1969, aged twenty-one. In 1981, she was shot in her home by members of the UDA but survived. She currently is a leading figure in the South Tyrone Empowerment Programme (STEP), which provides support for migrant workers.

Background

At the time I was growing up, politics weren't part of the conversation in any decent person's house. That was the kind of thinking – people didn't discuss contentious things. But ours was a very political house in other ways. My father was an avid trade unionist, a member of the Amalgamated Woodworkers' Union. He was educated through the Workers' Education Association, having left school to be a bicycle boy for a grocer's shop to pay off family debt and to contribute to the family income through goods in exchange for his labour on the bicycle. At fifteen he got paid five shillings to start an apprenticeship as a woodworker. He continued to work all his life until he died very young, at forty-six, when I was nine years of age. He was a highly political person, a self-read, self-educated man, who considered himself a trade unionist and a republican in a sense that republicanism has not understood post-1969/70. Not in terms of armed or not armed, which is how we tend to look at it, but a republican in the vein of Thomas Paine and a republican in the sense of republicanism separated out from Hibernianism.

But his republicanism was never overt. Implicit in the way we grew up were the core tenets of republicanism, not particularly applied to Ireland. It was about freedom of conscience, it was about responsibility for one's own actions. And there were words that we did know – 'usurpation' was a great word my father used, about the usurpation of rights. He had a very anti-imperialist position, so we grew up with that kind of radical thinking, but we didn't think of it as politics. That's the way my father was. You took responsibility for yourself, and you were as good as everybody else and better than nobody.

That tied in very much with my mother's more charismatic Catholic thinking. As we used to say, she was charismatic before post-Vatican II – before they invented it. She was a very broad-minded woman to have come out of a very small town. In a social sense, she was a very non-judgmental woman, much less judgmental than my father. I've said this many times: the only dispute that I remember in our house was on Easter Sunday, when my father produced the lilies and my mother complained about them. That was a ritual we knew as children. On Easter Sunday morning it was good coats on, lilies on, lilies off. Then the negotiation that the lilies wouldn't be put on until we got to the top of the road, so that we didn't offend the neighbours as we went out of the estate [*Laughs*]. When you got to the top of the road, then you were on a main road – it didn't belong to anybody. That was open territory, but to wear your lily up the estate was considered not fitting.

The Centenaries

I remember the fiftieth anniversary of the Easter Rising. My younger sister went on the school trip to Dublin for the anniversary, while I was already out of St Patrick's Academy and at Queen's University. Before that – before 1966 – in my last year at school, what had a bigger impact on me was *Mise Éire,* a film which was shown in the school on repeated occasions [*Laughs*].

I just thought it was a very powerful film. It had two effects on me. One was Ó Riada's music and, if you like, a rediscovery of traditional music. But it also made coherent for me what, as I say, was there by implication but hadn't been articulated. But that's not to say it then made me who I was. Following my father's and later my mother's death – she died when I was nineteen – most of my radical politics came from experience of the state's role in my own poverty, and seeing education as a way out of that. The time of the Easter Rising anniversary was not particularly important to me; at that point my mother was seriously ill and we were caught up in her deteriorating health and her death. My father died in 1956 and my mother died in 1967, January 1967. So the fiftieth anniversary wasn't impacting very much on me personally at the time. But I think it had a wider effect – all these commemorations do. They seep into the psyche of people.

As to the coming centenaries, there will be people who will want to say these are of no importance, there will be people who will want to say these are of the utmost significance, and there are people for whom they have no importance, for whom an importance will be contrived [*Laughs*]. All of those will be there. It's interesting to look at a comparison as to where the players in time have taken us, from 1916 to 2016. In 1916 we were on our way out of the empire, and in 2016 we're on our way back in. It will be interesting [*Laughs*]. I do believe that's the political thinking, and one which Sinn Féin, if not publicly articulating, is not averse to. That's just an opinion of mine, is that the rejoining of the British Commonwealth is not far off. Had the Queen not an inkling that she'd be getting her territory back, she wouldn't have set foot in the Republic of Ireland. The media bit has all been about 'us letting her come'. Let me tell you, royalty does not entertain that kind of nonsense. From Her Majesty's point of view, agreeing to set foot on Irish republican soil would not have happened if Article 2 of the constitution had not been dropped and if she didn't have an understanding of closer relationships. I think by the time we get to the hundredth anniversary of the Treaty, we'll be signing it.

The centenary in 2016 will not be allowed to put a brake on that. There'll be very little said about the ideals [*Laughs*]. I wouldn't imagine the ideals, as enunciated then, will get much of a look in – there are all kinds of reasons why that won't be the case. The symbolism, of course, the sacrifice, the nationalism will be highlighted. The different players are differently positioned, and each of them will make the running for how far we have come. There'll certainly be nobody on the anniversary of the 1916 Rising running a theme of 'What a parcel of rogues in a nation!' or 'It's a pity good men died for them.' I don't think that will be the theme of the celebrations. And I don't believe people are encouraged to think any more, so it's hard to know what would have a negative effect.

Because some people think – you know, that was part of the narrative – that '66 was what caused the conflict in the north. God love their wit. If that's where you want to take the narrative, then you have to be very careful that in 2016 you don't allow that to happen again. But if you're thinking was wrong about that, then does it really matter?

To ask if the ideals and beliefs of the men of 1916 have been realised is a simplistic question. You can't say yea or nay. The people involved in that struggle had their own different and very often conflicting visions of what would happen, not simply around 1916 but around the settlement. The Civil War in the south was fought basically over being master or mistress – but certainly at that time being master – of your own house, and having a sovereign republic as opposed to a dominion. And yet in the movement of global politics, the Republic of Ireland, now in hock to high-class gamblers, has probably less control over its affairs than at any time in the history of the formation of the state. So maybe it's two steps forward, three steps back. A hundred years after 1916 might be a timely opportunity to reflect on those matters, but they'll not be reflected on. There'll be great drumming up, there will be the traditional queuing and vying for ownership of the Garden of Remembrance. There will be claim and counter-claim. Brian Moore had a song on Michael Collins – 'Hang Out Your Brightest Colours' – a great song. Everybody will want to claim the bits they want of those who fought the Rising. People will want to claim the courage of those who died at the Somme. But there'll be nobody reflecting on, 'Did anybody learn anything which takes us forward?' That won't be happening. These commemorations are never about reflection, about evaluation, about recommitment to any ideals. They are about marking out ownership of narratives and territory.

If I suddenly had magical control of commemoration, the first thing I would discourage would be anybody assembling simply for the purpose of saying, 'I wasn't there at the time.' As an avid marcher and demonstrator, I think people need to assemble in the streets with purpose and intent, to change the status quo. To assemble in the street simply to claim the past is to my mind a tyranny, because the past cannot belong to the present. It can't – any more than the future can belong to the past. And I think that that kind of action is always limiting of the present. I know it's a very hard thing to say, but it is reality and I suppose it's reality that comes to me through the kind of republicanism that my father believed in: that the dead cannot dictate the present. The dead are dead – they have no stake in it, they're not here. They can inform – the past can inform and guide us in our thinking in the present – but we can't make choices in the present because somebody died at the Somme or because somebody died in the Easter Rising or because somebody signed the Covenant in his blood. We can understand and learn from why they did, we can try to extract from that something that will guide us to a better humanity in the future, but we can't say, 'We're not allowed to do this because somebody died for something else.'

Humanising the people who died – that's another great word. Humanising tends to be used in some way to trivialise them, to point them out as fundamentally flawed. That's not humanising them; it's trivialising them and it's demeaning them. If you want to humanise them, then let's not worry about whether Pádraig Pearse had a turn in his eye or not, let's have a look at what he said in *The Murder Machine* about education. And let's not taint our understanding of what he said there by the fact that he was one of 'them' and so we shouldn't listen to what he had to say.

The signing of the Covenant is the one that interests me most, and only because for me it has a practical use for the present and the future. In the Good Friday Agreement we were promised a Bill of Rights. It was going to be passed in Westminster for the purpose of sitting above the government here, and its function was to set out the basic principles of rights that we would all adhere to, so that we would never go back to where we had been. Now that development of a Bill of Rights, of a Charter, of a set of principles to which we sign our brotherhood and sisterhood, has resonance with me of a covenant. And since we haven't got a Bill of Rights from Westminster, and they're quite intent that we don't, I think we should begin to make our own covenant, based on the advice given from the Human Rights Commission. We as a people should begin from the community, the same as the covenanters did. If the government won't give the people a Bill of Rights, then the people should take from the government a Bill of Rights.

When I think of 'the people', I think first of all of me, myself and I – three very important people. And I never mistake that for 'we'. That's singular. Me, myself and I – I think, I want, I need, I know. I never confuse that for the royal 'we'. Then people grow from that. The people who matter to me after that are the people with whom I live and work, so when I talk about people I put them in terms of locations. Then if I talk about the Irish people, I'm talking about all the people on this island. But in the context of what I've just said, on the covenant and the Bill of Rights, that only applies within the north.

I also think there is a piece of work to be done around the original constitution. One of the things we might do in terms of preparing for 2016 is begin a similar constitutional exercise in the south, about a constitution that is fit for people in the twenty-first century and the second century of the state. Now I think if we were doing that in the modern context, the only real framework that we have to build on is the United Nations framework of human rights, because that doesn't require us to be Loyalists or republicans or Irish or British or Portuguese – it requires us to be human beings, and to accord to other human beings the rights we would want for ourselves. So those are two different starting points which can take us to the same shared place, based on real shared values and not on negotiated common prejudices against somebody else.

Much has been made of the fact that there's been a shift in the thinking in the south about the Irish participation in the Battle of the Somme, and I think that again is a constructed narrative. When you talk about going back to my childhood, I still remember all the songs I learnt in my own home that related to Suvla Bay, and not simply the Irish songs of the people who didn't go there, but of the people who did. Because in the real communities of real people, real grandfathers and real fathers died there, and they were never ever, ever forgotten. Never forgotten. My mother bought poppies when we were children. We had Easter Lilies on Sunday, and we bought poppies. The argument reversed then as to whether we would wear them or not, because though it didn't offend our neighbours to wear them, it offended our father to wear them! [*Laughs*] He was anti-imperialism and he saw the First World War as an imperialist war.

I think the Battle of the Somme sits with the Hunger Strike in my psyche. It was such a terrible, terrible thing to happen. Why do we seek to glorify it all the time? People died. There seemed at the time to be no way to stop all that happening, and no way to get a good outcome out of that. The amount of human life wasted at the Somme …

That isn't to say that the people who went there weren't brave. But not very many people who went to the Somme knew what the Somme was going to be like the day they headed out. And not many people who went into the civil rights movement and into the republican movement, and into the prisons, knew what it was going to be like the day they headed out. Those are real heartaches for real people. But the construction of this narrative that the Irish who died at the Somme were forgotten? Just because *you* forgot about them doesn't mean everybody else did; just because *you* didn't know doesn't mean everybody else didn't. To say that because the state didn't do something means that there was shame – that is a lie. It's a constructed narrative and a lie. Tom Hartley can come out and talk about his own people – he didn't discover that yesterday. He always knew it. But it now it is safe enough to say it out loud. But don't blame us for that. Don't blame those of us who have complex lives for the narrow simplicity of constructed narratives.

Public commemoration matters if we make it matter. And that's what I mean when I say people are manipulated into saying things. It's now the done thing for all of us, since Princess Diana died – it's our moral responsibility to weep for the wealthy we never met, as if our mother reared them [*Laughs*]. How do we learn from the Battle of the Somme and not take Iraq and Afghanistan and Libya into the equation? Never mind the rights or wrongs of it, think of it in terms of the individual people. The man in the street who stood in line in Libya and fought the NATO tanks – whatever Gaddafi was – was the same as the soldier at the Somme who laid his life on the line for tyrants on every side. So how come it's good enough to trail their bodies through the street in the twenty-first century and at the same time create some sainthood for people in exactly the same position a hundred years ago?

To ask if we live in a post-nationalist era and a globalised world is to ask the wrong question, in terms of what sovereignty actually means. Again it takes us, at the end of the conversation, back to the beginning of the conversation. The debate between Thomas Paine and Edmund Burke is as valid today as it ever was. It was fundamentally a debate around what constitutes sovereignty. Burke, who was an Irishman and an English nationalist, laid the foundations of nationalist ideology by bedding that in the state and government. So once the nation becomes the state, then the people have no say. It was Paine who said no, the nation is the people and the state is the government. And the nation will always be changing. Sovereignty has to be in the hands of the people.

Then we come, interestingly enough, to the present situation in Greece, where the Greek Prime Minister is absolutely right. This decision about the degree of debt and the degree of austerity for these people is one that every adult must append their signature to, for or against. That's what a republic is. And that's what I say about the Good Friday Agreement and about Article 2 of the constitution. Don't whinge to me about it, because I didn't vote for either. I thought they were both bad deals. But they were held up by referendum. Don't blame Gerry Adams, don't blame Martin McGuinness, don't blame Peter Robinson – you all, every adult here, appended your personal responsibility to this. And to say now, 'I didn't know what I was signing,' is a disgrace for you who signed it, because that is what it's about – it's about people taking responsibility for what they do. So if we are talking about sovereignty, then we're talking about people being able to participate, knowledgeably and informed, and take responsibility for decision-making. Otherwise we're not adults. That's what makes us adults: that we take decisions, we take informed decisions, and we take responsibility for the decisions we take and their consequences.

In the context of the whole island? We've never had an all-island referendum. But the questions were posed in parallel – that the people of the north voted for the Good Friday Agreement and the people of the south … well, of course we never put Article 2 in. We never voted for the constitution, we never voted for any of it. But that's what Article 2 was mindful about, and Article 2 set out that the state was smaller than the nation. That's all it did. It acknowledged that the state was smaller than the nation and in taking it away, that acknowledgement was taken away. The people of the south took it away. I think that was a very significant thing to do and they bear a responsibility for that. I don't think the Queen would have gone there had they not done it.

But I think the jury is out on what the physical infrastructure of sovereignty will look like on this island or any other island. The process is what determines it. So we may end up with any number of things. The federated states of the British Isles? There may be two such states on this island, there may be one – who knows? We may end up going back into the Commonwealth and thereby, ironically, opening the door for reunification of the island. But those are the mechanics. My problem, taking us back to commemorations, is that we are obsessed with the mechanics and the commemorations, and we abandon ethics and principles and purpose.

Other titles published by The History Press

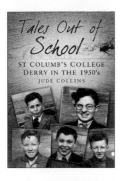

TALES OUT OF SCHOOL: ST COLUMB'S COLLEGE IN THE 1950s
JUDE COLLINS

St Columb's College, Derry, produced two Nobel Laureates in Seamus Heaney and John Hume, but in this fascinating collection of interviews Jude Collins looks behind the scenes at the unsung, unseen majority that made up real life in this remarkable institution.

978 1 84588 983 8

PRESIDENT MARY MCALEESE: BUILDING BRIDGES
MARY MCALEESE

From 1997 to 2011, Mary McAleese served as President of Ireland, and became one of the most popular Presidents this country has ever known. Representing Ireland on the world stage through the highs of the Celtic Tiger and the lows of recent years, she has sounded a voice that is trusted and respected and has become one of the finest examples of what Ireland could and should be. This book contains the key speeches from her time in office.

978 1 84588 724 7

CHIEFS OF STAFF:
THE PORTRAIT COLLECTION OF THE IRISH DEFENCE FORCES
EDITED BY COL. TOM HODSON

The Defence Forces Headquarters Mess in McKee Barracks, Dublin, houses a unique collection of portraits of all the Chiefs of Staff. An exceptional record of leadership, it contains many works by the most notable Irish portrait painters from the 1950s to the present day. This book reproduces the collection with superb full-colour images of the paintings, each accompanied by detailed entries on the Chief-of-Staff's career and that of the artist.

978 1 84588 755 1

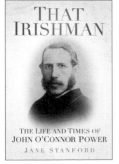

THAT IRISHMAN: THE LIFE AND WORK OF JOHN O'CONNOR POWER
JANE STANFORD

The story of John O'Connor Power is the story of Ireland's struggle for nationhood. Born into poverty, he rose through the ranks of the Fenian Movement to the Supreme Council of the Irish Republican Brotherhood. Elected to the House of Commons, he was acknowledged as one of the outstanding orators of his day. His speeches inspired the foundation of one of Ireland's most powerful political forces, the Land League. In short, he helped to make the dream of an independent Ireland a reality.

978 1 84588 698 1

Visit our websites and discover thousands of other History Press books.

www.thehistorypress.ie www.thehistorypress.co.uk